POLITICS AND POLICIES OF INTERNATIONAL RELATIONS

Politics and Policies of International Relations

A.K. Dixit

CYBER TECH PUBLICATIONS
4264/3, Ansari Road, Daryaganj, New Delhi-110002 (India)
Ph.: 011-23244078. Fax: 011-23280028
E-Mail: cyberpublicationsdelhi@yahoo.com

Politics and Policies of International Relations

First Edition 2009

Published by G.S. Rawat
For Cyber Tech Publications
4264/3, Ansari Road, Daryaganj, New Delhi - 110 002
E-mail : cyberpublicationsdelhi@yahoo.com
Phone : 011-23244078,
Fax : 011-23280028

Printed at
Amit Enterprises, Moujpur, Delhi. Ph. - 9810878184

Preface

India is a peace loving country. Truth and non-violence have always been the important features of our foreign policy since times immorial. We believe in the policy "Peace at home and Peace abroad" and doctrine of "Live and Let live."

Many important questions in the study of international relations are connected with the theory and practice of sovereign statehood which, as indicated, is the central historical institution of world politics. But there are other important issues as well. That has led to ongoing debates about the proper scope of international relations. At one extreme the scholarly focus is exclusively on states and interstate relations; but at another extreme international relations includes almost everything that has to do with human relations across the world. It is important to study these different perspectives if we hope to have a balanced and rounded knowledge of International Relations.

We record our grateful acknowledgments to national and international scholars and institutions, for excellent contributions on the subject.

My publisher and his staffmembers have assisted in every possible ways and have worked hard for its timely completion of this book.

—Editor

Contents

1

An Introducton to International Relations

Relations between politically organised human groupings which occupy distinctive territories, are not under any higher authority or power, and enjoy and exercise a measure of independence from each other. Security, freedom, order, justice, and welfare. Major traditional International Relations approaches, realism, liberalism and international Society. A doctrine and an arrangement whereby the power of one state (or group of states) is checked by the countervailing power of other states. International relation is the study of the nature and consequences of these relations. On the contrary, they adjoin each other and affect each other and must therefore somehow find ways to coexist and to deal with each other. They are usually embedded in international markets which affect the policies of their governments and the wealth and welfare of their citizens. That requires that they enter into relations with each other. Complete isolation is usually not an option. When states are isolated and are cut off from the state system, either by their own government or by foreign powers, the people usually suffer as a result. That has been the situation recently with regard to Burma, Libya, Iraq, and Iran. The state system is a system of social relations, that is, a system of relations between groups of human beings. Like most other social systems, international relations can have certain advantages and disadvantages for the participants. The state system is a distinctive way of organising political life on earth which has deep historical roots. There have been state systems or quasi-state systems at different times and places in different parts of the world for example, in ancient India, in ancient Greece and in Renaissance Italy.

However, the subject of inernational relations conventionally dates back to the early modern era (sixteenth and seventeenth centuries) in Europe, when sovereign states based on adjacent territories were initially established. Ever since the eighteenth century the relations between such Independent states have been labelled international relations'. In the nineteenth and twentieth centuries the state system was expanded to encompass the entire territory of the earth. The world of states is basically a territorial world; it is a way of politically organising the world's populated territory, a distinctive kind of territorial political organisation which is based on numerous different governments that are legally independent of each other. The only large territory that is not a state is Antarctica, and it is administered by a consortium of states.

These are social values that are so fundamental to human well-being that they must be protected or ensured in some way. That could be by social organisations other than the state. e.g., by family, clan, ethnic or religious organisations. In the modern era, however, the state has usually been involved as the leading institution in that regard: it is expected to insure these basic values. For example, people generally assume that the state should and will underwrite the value of national security, which involves the protection of citizens from internal and external threat. That is a fundamental concern or interest of states. However, the very existence of independent states affects the value of security; we live in a world of many states almost all of which are armed at least to some degree. Thus states can both defend and threaten peoples' security, and that paradox of the state system is usually referred to as the security dilemma.' In other words, just like any other human organisation, states present problems as well as provide solutions. Most states are likely to be friendly non-threatening and peace-loving. But a few states may be hostile and aggressive and there is not world government to constrain them. That poses a basic and age-old problem of state systems: national security. To deal with that problem most states possess armed forces. Military power is usually considered a necessity so that states can coexist and deal with each other without being intimidated or subjugated. Unarmed states are extremely rare in the history of the state system. That is a basic fact of the state system that we should never lose sight of. Many states also enter into alliances with other states to increase their national security. To ensure that no great power succeeds in achieving a hegemonic position of overall dominations, based on intimidation, coercion, or the outright use of force, it is also necessary to constract and maintain a balance of military power. Security is obviously one of the most fundamental values of international relations. That approach to the study of world politics is typical of realist theories of International Relations.

It operates on the assumption that relations of states can be best characterised as a world in which armed states are competing rivals and periodically go to war with each other. The second basic value that states are usually expected to uphold is freedom, both personal freedom and national freedom or independence. A fundamental reason for having states and putting up with the burdens that governments place on citizens, such as tax burdens or obligations of military service, is the condition of national freedom or independence of which states exist to foster. We cannot be free unless our country is free too; that was made very clear to millions of Czech, Polish, Danish, Norweigian, Belgian, and Dutch citizens as well as citizens of other countries that were invaded and occupied by Nazi Germany during the Second World War. Even if our country is free we may still not be free personally, but at least then the problem of our freedom is in our own hands. War threatens and sometimes destroys freedom. Peace fosters freedom. Peace also makes progressive international change possible, that is, the creation of a better world. Peace and progressive change are obviously among the most fundamental values of international relations. That approach to the study of world politics is typical of liberal theories of international relations. It operates on the assumption that international relations can be best characterised as a world in which states cooperate with each other to maintain peace and freedom and to pursue progressive change.

The third and fourth basic values that states are usually expected to uphold are order and justice. States have a common interest in establishing and maintaining international order so that they can coexist and interact on a basis of stability, certainty, and predictability. To that end, states are expected to uphold international law; to keep their treaty commitments and to observe the rules, conventions, and customs of the international legal order. They are also expected to follow accepted practices of diplomacy and to support international organisations. International law, diplomatic relations and international organisations can only exist and operate successfully if these expectations are generally met by most states most of the time. States are also expected to uphold human rights. Today there is an elaborate international legal framework of human rights—civil, political, social, and economic—which has been developed since the end of the Second World War. Order and justice obviously are among the most fundamental values of international relations. That approach to the study of world politics is typical of International Society theories of IR (Bull 1995). It operates on the assumption that international relations can be best characterised as a world in which states are socially responsible actors and have a common interest in preserving international order and promoting international justice.

The final basic value that states are usually expected to uphold is the population's socioeconomic wealth and welfare. People expect their government to adopt appropriate policies to encourage high employment, low inflation steady investment, the uninterrupted flow of trade and commerce, and so forth. Because national economies are rarely isolated from each other, most people also expect that the state will respond to the international economic environment in such a way as to enhance or at least defend and maintain the national standard of living.

States nowadays try to frame and implement economic policies that can maintain the stability of the international economy upon which they are all increasingly dependent. That usually involves economic policies that can deal adequately with international markets, with the economic policies of other states, with foreign investment, with foreign exchange rates, with international trade, with international transportation and communications, and with other international economic relations that affect national wealth and welfare. Economic interdependence, meaning a high degree of mutual economic dependence among countries, is a striking feature of the contemporary state system. Some people consider that to be a good thing because it may increase overall freedom and wealth by expanding the global marketplace and thereby increasing participation, specialisation, efficiency, and productivity. Other people consider it to be a bad thing because it may promote overall inequality by allowing rich and powerful countries, or countries with financial or technological advantages, to dominate poor and weak countries that lack those advantages. But either way wealth and welfare obviously are among the most fundamental values of international relations. That approach to the study of world politics is typical of (international political economy theories of international relations. It operates on the assumption that international relations can be best characterised as fundamentally a socioeconomic world and not merely a political and military world.

They only become aware of them when something goes wrong—for example, during a war or a depression, when things begin to get beyond the control of individual states. On those learning occasions people wake up to the larger circumstances of their lives which in normal times are a silent or invisible background. At those moments they are likely to become sharply aware of what they take for granted, and of how important these values really are in their everyday lives. We become aware of national security when a foreign power rattles its saber or engages in hostile actions against our country or one of our allies. We become aware of national independence and our freedom as citizens when peace is no longer guaranteed. We become aware of international order and justice when some states, especially major powers, abuse, exploit, denounce, or disregard international law or trample on human rights. We become aware of national welfare and our own personal socioeconomic well-being when foreign countries or international investors use their economic clout to jeopardise our standard of living.

The First World War made it dreadfully clear to most people just how devastatingly destructive of lives and living conditions modern mechanised warfare between major powers can be, and just how important it is to reduce the risk of great power war. That recognition led to the first major developments of international relations thought which tried to find effective legal institutions—e.g., the Covenant of the League of Nations—to prevent great-power war. The Great Depression brought home to many people around the world how their economic livelihood could be adversely affected, in some cases destroyed, by conditions and events in other countries. The Second World War not only underlined the reality of the dangers of great-power war but also revealed how important it is to prevent any great power from getting out of control and how unwise it is to pursue a policy of appeasement—which was adopted by Britain and France in regard to Nazi Germany just prior to the war with disastrous consequences for every body, including the German people. There have also been moments of heightened awareness of the fundamental importance of these values since the end of the Second World War.

The Cuban missile crisis of 1963 brought home to many people the dangers of nuclear war. The anti-colonial movements in Asia and Africa of the 1950s and 1960s and the secessionist movements in the former Soviet Union and former Yugoslavia at the end of the Cold War made it clear how important self-determination and political independence continue to be. The global inflation of the 1970s and early 1980s caused by a sudden dramatic increase in oil price by the OPEC cartel of oil-exporting countries was a reminder of how the interconnectedness of the global economy can be a threat to national and personal welfare anywhere in the world. For example, the oil shock of the 1970s made it abundantly clear to countless American, European and Japanese motorists—among others—that economic policies of Middle-East and other major oil producing countries could suddenly raise the price of gas or petrol at the pump and lower their standard of living. The Gulf War (1990-91) and the conflicts in the Balkans (1992-95) were a reminder of the importance of international order and respect for human rights. For a long time there has been a basic assumption that life inside properly organized and well managed states is better than life outside states or without states at all. For example, the jews spent more than half a century trying to get a state of their own in which they could be secure: Israel. As long as states and the state system manage to maintain the foregoing core values, that assumption holds. That has generally been the case for developed countries, especially the states of Western Europe, North American, Japan, Australia, New Zealand, and some others. That gives rise to more conventional international relations theories which regard the state system as a valuable core institution of modern life. The traditional international relations theories discussed in this book tend to adopt that positive view. They recognize the significance of these basic values even if they disagree about which ones are most important—e.g., realists emphasise the importance of security and order, liberals emphasize freedom and justice, and IPE scholars emphasize economic equality and welfare.

But if states are not successful in that regard the state system can easily be understood in the opposite light not as upholding basic social conditions and values, but rather as undermining them. That is the case with regard to many states in the third World especially sub-Saharan Africa. It is also the case with regard to some states which emerged as a result of the breakup of the Soviet Union and Yugoslavia at the end of the Cold War. Many of these states more or less fail to provide or protect even to a minimal standard at least some of the five basic values discussed above. More than a few states fail to ensure any of them. The plight of countless men, women and children in those countries puts into question the credibility and perhaps even the legitimacy of the state system. It promotes a corresponding assumption that the international system fosters or at least tolerates human suffering, and that the system should be changed so that people everywhere can flourish, and not just those in the developed countries of the world. That gives rise to more critical international relations theories which regard the state and the state system as a less beneficial and more problematical institution.

The alternative international relations theories discussed later in this book tend to adopt that critical view. To sum up thus far states and the system of states are territory-based social organisations which exist primarily to establish, maintain, and defend basic social conditions and values, including particularly security, freedom, order, justice, and welfare. These are the main reasons for having states. Many states and certainly all developed countries uphold these conditions and values at least to minimal standards and often at a higher level. Indeed, they have been so successful in doing that for the past several centuries that the standards have steadily increased and are now higher than every. These countries set the international standard for the entire world. But many states and most under developed countries fail to meet even minimal standards, and as a consequence their presence in the contemporary state system raises serious questions not only about those states but also about the state system of which they are an important part.

It is important to emphasise that the state system is a historical institution. It is not ordained by God or determined by Nature. It has been fashioned by people: it is a social organisation. Like all social organisations, the state system has certain advantages and certain disadvantages which change over time. There is nothing about the state system that is necessary to human existence, even though there may be many things about it that are advantageous to high standards of living. But people have not always lived in sovereign states. For most of human history people have organised their political lives in different ways, the most common being that of political empire such as the Roman empire. In the future the world may not be organised into a state system either. People may eventually give up on sovereign statehood and abandon the institution. People throughout history have abandoned many other ways of organising their political lives, including city-states, feudalism, and colonialism, to mention of few. It is not unreasonable to suppose that a form of global political organisation that is better or more advanced than states and the state system will eventually be adopted. Some IR scholars discussed in later chapters believe that such an international transformation, connected with growing interdependence among states (i.e. globalisation), is already well under way. But the state system has been a central institution of world politics for a very long time and still remains so. Even though world politics is in flux, in the past states and the state system have always managed to adapt to significant historical change. But nobody can be sure that that will continue to be the case in the future. This issue of present and future international change is discussed later in the chapter.

There were no clearly recognisable sovereign states before the sixteenth century when they first began to be instituted in Western Europe. But for the past three or four centuries, states and the system of states have structured the political lives of an every increasing number of people around the world. They have become universally popular. Today the system is global in extent. The era of the sovereign state coincides with the modern age of expanding power, prosperity, knowledge, science, technology, literacy, urbanisation, citizenship, freedom, equality, rights, etc. This could be a coincidence, but that is not very likely when we remember how important states and the state system have been in shaping the five fundamental human values discussed above. Of course, it is difficult to say whether states were the effect or the cause of modern life, and whether they will have any place in a postmodern age. Those questions must be set aside for later.

However, we do know that the state system and modernity are closely related historically. In fact, they are completely coexistent; the system of adjoining territorial states arose in Europe at the start of the modern era. And the state system has been a central if not a defining feature of modernity ever since. Although the sovereign state emerged in Europe, it extended to North America in the late eighteenth century and to South America in the early nineteenth century. As modernity spread around the world the state system spread with it. Only slowly did it expand to cover the entire globe. Sub-Saharan Africa, for example, remained isolated from the expanding Western state system until the late nineteenth century, and it only became an independent regional state system after the middle of the twentieth century. Whether the end of modernity will also bring the end of the state system is an important question that must be left for later in this book. Of course, there is evidence of political systems that resembled sovereign states long before the modern age. They obviously had relations of some sort with each other. The historical origin of international relations in that more general sense lies deep in history and can only be a matter of speculation. But, speaking conceptually, it was a time when people began to settle down on the land and form themselves into separate territory-based political communities. The first examples of that date back more than 5,000 years.Each political group faced the inescapable problem of coexisting with neighbouring groups whom they could not ignore or avoid because they were right there next door. Each political grouping also had to deal with groups that were further away but were still capable of affecting them. Their geographical closeness must have come to be regarded as a zone of political proximity, if not a frontier or border of some kind. Where group contact occurred, sometimes it must have involved rivalry, disputes, threats, intimidation, intervention, invasion, conquest, and other hostile and warlike interactions. But sometimes and perhaps most of the time, it must also have involved mutual respect, cooperation, commerce, conciliation, dialogue, and similar friendly and peaceful relations. A very significant form of dialogue between autonomous political communities—diplomacy—has ancient roots.

There are recorded formal agreements among ancient political communities which date as far back as 1390 BC, and records of quasi-diplomatic activity as early as 653 BC Barber 1979: 8-9). Here in prototype is the classical problem of IR: war and peace, conflict and cooperation. Here, too, are the different aspects of international relations emphasised by realism and liberalism.

These relations between independent political groups make up the core problem of international relations. They are built on a fundamental distinction between our collective selves and other collective selves in a territorial world of many such separate collective selves in contact with each other. Here, we arrive at a preliminary definition of a 'state system': it stands for relations between politically organised human groupings which occupy distinctive territories, are not under any higher authority or power, and enjoy and exercise a measure of independence from each other. International relations are relations between such independent groups. The first relatively clear historical manifestation of a state system is that of ancient Greece (500 BC –100 BC), then known as *Hellas*. It comprised a large number of mostly small city-states (Weight (1977; Watson 1992). Ancient Greece was not a nation-state the way it is today. Rather, it was a system of city states. Athens was the largest and most famous, but there were also many other city states, such as Sparta and Corinth. Together they formed the first state system in Western history. There were extensive and elaborate relations between the city states of Hellas. But the ancient Greek city states were not modern sovereign states with extensive territories. They were far smaller in population and territory than most modern states. Greek intercity relations also lacked the institution of diplomacy, and there was nothing comparable to international law and international organisation.

The ancient Greek state system was eventually destroyed by more powerful neighbouring empires, and in due course the Greeks became subjects of the Roman Empire (200 BC-500 AD). The Romans developed a huge empire in the course of conquering, occupying, and ruling most of Europe and a large part of the Middle East and North Africa. The Romans had to deal with the numerous political communities that occupied these areas, but they did that by subordinating them rather than recognising them. Instead of international relations or quasi-international relations, under the Roman empire the only option for political communities was either submission to Rome or revolt. Eventually those communities on the periphery of the empire began to revolt; the Roman army could not contain the revolts and began to retreat, and on several occasions the city of Rome itself was invaded and shattered by the barbarian' tribes. In that way the Roman empire was finally brought to an end after many centuries of political success and survival.

Empire was the prevalent pattern of political organisation that gradually emerged in Christian Europe over several centuries after the fall of the Roman empire. Rome's two main successors in Europe also were empires; in Western Europe the medieval (Catholic empire based at Rome (Christendom); in Eastern Europe and the near east the Byzantine (Orthodox) empire centred on Constantinople or what is today Istanbul (Byzantium) Byzantium claimed to be the continuation of the Christianized Roman empire. The European medieval Christian world (500-1500) was thus divided geographically most of the time into two politico-religious empires. There were other political systems and empires further North African and other civilisations. There were empires in what is today Iran and India. The oldest empire was the Chinese which survived, under different dynasties, for about 4,000 years until the early twentieth century. Perhaps it still exists in the form of the Chinese Communist state, which resembles an empire in its hierarchical political and ideological structure the Middle Ages were thus an era of empire and the relations and conflicts of different empires. But contact between empires was intermittent at best: communications were slow and transportation was difficult. Most empires at that time consequently were a world unto themselves.

Can we speak of international relations' in Western Europe during the medieval era? Only with difficulty because, as already indicated, medieval Christendom was more like an empire than a state system. States existed, but they were not independent or sovereign in the modern meaning of these words. There were no clearly defined territories with borders. The medieval world was not a geographical patchwork of sharply differentiated colours which represented different independent countries. Instead, it was a complicated and confusing intermingling of lines and colours of varying shades and hues. Power and authority were organised on both a religious and a political basis; the Pope and the Emperor were the heads of two parallel and connected hierarchies, one religious and the other political. Kings and other rulers were subjects of those higher authorities and their laws. They were not fully independent. And much of the time local rulers were more or less free from the rule of kings; they were semi autonomous but they were not fully independent either. The fact is that territorial political independence as we know it today was not present in medieval Europe.

Sometimes wars were fought between kings—for example, the Hundred Years War between England and France (1337-

1453). But often war was feudal and local and was fought between rival groups of knights whose leaders had a quarrel. The authority and power to engage in war was not monopolised by the state: kings did not control war as they were later able to do. Instead, war-making rights and capacities belonged to members of a distinctive caste—the armed knights and their leaders and followers—who fought sometimes for the Pope, sometimes for the Emperor, sometimes for their king, sometimes for their master, and sometimes and indeed quite regularly for themselves. There was no clear distinction between civil war and international war. Medieval wars were more likely to be fought over issues of rights and wrongs; wars to defend the faith, wars to resolve conflicts over dynastic inheritance, wars to punish outlaws, wars to collect debts, etc. (Howard 1976: ch. 1). Wars were less likely to be fought over the exclusive control of territory or over state or national interests. In medieval Europe there was no exclusively controlled territory, and no clear conception of the nation or the national interest.

The values connected with sovereign statehood were arranged differently in medieval times. The key to that difference is the fact that no one political organisation, such as the sovereign state, catered for all these values. Instead, they were looked after by different organisations which operated at different levels of social life. Security was provided by local rulers and their knights who operated from fortified castles and towns. Freedom was not freedom for the individual or the nation; rather, it was freedom for feudal rulers and their followers and clients. Order was the responsibility of the emperor but his capacity to enforce order was very limited and medieval Europe was punctuated by turbulence and discord at all levels of society. The provision of justice was the responsibility of both political and religious rulers, but it was a highly unequal justice. Those higher up in the political and religious hierarchies had easier access to justice than those at the bottom. There were different courts for different classes of people. There was no police, and often justice was meted out by people themselves in the form of revenge or reprisal. The Pope was responsible not only for ruling the Church through his hierarchy of bishops and other clergy but also for overseeing political disputes between kings and other semi-independent national rulers. Members of the clearly were often senior advisers to kings and other secular rulers. Kings were sometimes "Defenders of the Faith'—such as Henry VIII of England. Knights often thought of themselves as Christian soldiers. Welfare was connected to security and was based on feudal ties between local rulers and common people in which those rulers provided protection in exchange for a share of the labour, crops and other resources and products of a local peasant economy. Peasants were not free to live wherever they wished. Instead, they were tied to feudal landlords who could be members of the nobility or the clergy or both.

What did the political change from medieval to modern basically involve? The short answer is: it eventually consolidated the provision of these values within the single framework of one united and independent social organisation: the sovereign state. In the early modern era European rulers liberated themselves from the overarching religious-political authority of Christendom. They also freed themselves from their dependence on the military power of barons and other local feudal leaders. The kings subordinated the barons and defied the emperor and the Pope. They became defenders of state sovereignty against internal disorder and external threat. Peasants began their long journey to escape from their dependence on local feudal rulers to become the direct subjects of the King: they eventually became 'the people'.

In short, power and authority were concentrated at one point: the King and his government. The King now ruled a territory with borders which were defended against outside interference. The King became the supreme authority over all the people in the country, and no longer had to operate via intermediate authorities and rulers.

That fundamental political transformation marks the advent of the modern era. One of the major effects of the rise of the modern state was its monopoly of the means of warfare. The King first created order at home and became the sole centre of power within the country. Knights and barons who had formerly controlled their own armies now took orders from the King. Many Kings then looked outward with an ambition to expand their territories. As a result international rivalries developed which often resulted in wars and the enlargement of some countries at the expense of others. At various times Spain, France, Austria, England, Denmark, Sweden, Holland, Poland, Russia, Prussia and other states of the new European state system were at war. Some wars were spawned by the Protestant Reformation which profoundly divided the European Christian population in the sixteenth and seventeenth centuries. But other wars, and increasingly most wars, were provoked by the mere existence of independent states whose rulers resorted to war as a means of defending their interests, pursuing their ambitions and, if possible, expanding their territorial holdings. War became a key international institution for resolving conflicts between sovereign states.

The political change from medieval to modern thus basically involved the construction of the independent territorial state. The state captured its territory and turned it into state property, and it captured the population of that territory and turned them into subjects and later citizens. In many countries, indeed most, the Christian churches fell under state control. There was no room within modern states for semi-independent territory or people or institutions. In the modern international system territory is consolidated, unified, and centralised under a sovereign government. The population of the territory owe their allegiance to that government and they have a duty to obey its laws. That includes bishops as well as barons, merchants as well as aristocrats. All institutions are now subordinate to state authority and public law. The familiar territorial patchwork map of the world in a place in which each patch is under the excusive jurisdiction of a particular state. All of the territory of Europe and eventually the entire planet is partitioned in that way by independent governments.

The historical end point of the medieval era and the starting-point of the modern international system, speaking very generally, is usually identified with the Thirty Years War (1018-48) and the Peace of Westphalia which brought it to an end. From the middle of the seventeenth century states were seen as the only legitimate political systems of Europe based on their own separate territories, their own independent governments, and their own political subjects. That emergent state system had several prominent characteristics which can be summarized. First, it consisted of adjoining states whose legitimacy and independence was mutually recognised. Second, that recognition of states did not extend outside of the European state system. Non-European political systems were not members of the state system. They were usually regarded as politically inferior and most of them were eventually subordinated to European imperial rule. Third, the relations of European states were subject to international law and diplomatic practices. In other words, they were expected to observe the rules of the international game Fourth, there was a balance of power between member states which was intended to prevent any one state from getting out of control and making a successful bid for hegemony which would in effect re-establish an empire over the continent.

There were several major attempts by different powers to impose their political hegemony on the continent. The Habsburg empire (Austria) made the attempt during the Thirty Years War (1618-1648), and was blocked by a coalition led by France and Sweden. France made the attempt under King Louis XIV (1661-1714) and was blocked by an English-Dutch alliance. Napoleon (1795-1815) made the attempt and was blocked by Britain, Russia Prussia, and Austria. A post-napolenoic balance of power among the great powers (the Concert of Europe) held for most of the period between 1815 and 1914. Germany made the attempt under Hitler (1939-45) and was blocked by the United States, the Soviet Union, and Britain. For the past 350 years the European state system had managed to resist the main political tendency of world history, which is the attempt by strong powers to bend weaker powers to their political will and thereby establish an empire.

The World Economy

The Western states that could not dominate each other succeeded in dominating much of the rest of the world both politically and economically. That outward control of the non-European world by Europeans began at the start of the early modern era in the sixteenth century, at the same time that the European state system was coming into existence. It lasted down to the middle of the twentieth century, when the last non-Western peoples finally broke free of Western colonialism and acquired political independence. The fact that Western states were never able to dominate each other but were entirely capable of dominating almost everybody else has been crucially important in shaping the modern international system.

The global ascendancy and supremacy of the West is crucial for understanding IR even today. The history of modern Europe is a history of political and economic conflict and war between its sovereign states. States made war, and war made and unmade states (Tilly 1992). European state rivalries were conducted not only in Europe but wherever European ambitions and power cold be projected—and that was, eventually, throughout the world. European states entered into competition with each other to penetrate and control militarily useful and economically desirable areas in other parts of the world. European states felt they had every right to do that. The idea that non-Western peoples had rights of independence and self-determination only came much later. Huge non-European territories and populations consequently fell under the control of European states, by military conquest, commercial domination, or political annexation. Western imperial expansion made possible for the first time the formation and operation of a global economy (Parry 1966) and a global polity (Bull and Watson 1984). The expansion of trade between the Western world and the non-Western world began at about the same time that the modern state was emerging in Europe—around they year 1500. That expansion was based on the long-distance and heavily armed sailing-ship which Europeans used both for transporting goods and for projecting military and political power. By such means European states expanded their power far beyond Europe.

The American continents were gradually brought into the world trading system via the mining of silver and other precious metals, the trade in furs, and the production of agricultural commodities—much of it produced on large plantations by slave labour. About the same time the East Indies and then continental parts of South Asia and South-East Asia came under European colonization and control. While the Spanish, the Portuguese, the Dutch, the English, and the French expanded their empires overseas, the Russians expanded theirs overland. By the late eighteenth century the Russian empire based on the fur trade extended across Siberia, into Alaska, and down the west coast of North America as far as northern California. The Western powers also forced the opening of trade with China and Japan—although neither country was colonised politically. Large territories of the non-European world were settled by Europeans and later became independent member states of the state system under the control of their settler populations; the United States, the states of Latin America, Canada, Australia, New Zealand and—for a long time—South Africa. The Middle East and tropical Africa were the last continents that Europeans colonised.

During the era of economic and political imperialism by European states a few fundamental points should be kept in mind which shed light on the state system at that time. First, European states made expedient alliances with non-European political systems—such as the alliances arranged by the British and by the French with different Indian 'tribes' (i.e. nations) of North America. Second, almost wherever they could, European states conquered and colonised those non-Western political systems and made them a subordinate part of their empires. Third, those far-flung empires became a basic source of the wealth and power of the European states for several centuries. Thus the development of Europe was achieved in significant part on the basis of the control of extensive territories outside Europe and by the exploitation of their natural and human resources. Fourth, some of those overseas colonies fell under the control of European settler populations, and many of those new 'settler states' were eventually allowed to become members of the state system. The successful American revolution against the British empire first opened that door in the late eighteenth century. That launched the transition from a European state system to a Western state system. Lastly, throughout the era of Western imperialism, from the sixteenth century until the early twentieth century, there was no interest or desire to incorporate non-Western political systems into the state system on a basis of equal sovereignty.

The first stage of the globalisation of the state system was via the incorporation of non-Western states that could not be colonised by the West. Not every non-Western country fell under the political control of a Western imperial state; but countries that escaped colonisation were still obliged to accept the rules of the Western state system.

China was obliged to accept the rules of the Western state system during the nineteenth and early twentieth century. China was not acknowledged and fully recognised as a great power until 1945. The second stage of the globalisation of the state system was brought about via anti-colonialism by the colonial subjects of Western empires. In that struggle indigenous political leaders made political claims for decolonisation and independence based on European and American ideas of self-determination. That 'revolt against the West', as Hedley Bull put it, was the main vehicle by which the state system expanded dramatically after the Second World War (Bull and Watson 1984). In a short period of some twenty years, beginning with the independence of India and Pakistan in 1947, most colonies in Asia and Africa became independent states and members of the United Nations. European decolonisation in the Third World more than tripled the membership of the UN from about 50 states in 1945 to over 160 states by 1970. About 70 per cent of the world's population were citizens or subjects of independents states in 1945 and were thus represented in the state system. By 1995 that figure was virtually 100 per cent.

The spread of European political and economic control beyond Europe thus eventually proved to be an expansion of the state system which became completely global in the second half of the twentieth century. The final stage of the globalisation of the state system was the dissolution of the Soviet Union together with the simultaneous breakup of Yugoslavia and Czechoslovakia at the end of the Cold War.

That expanded UN membership to about 190 states at the end of the twentieth century. Today the state system is a global institution that affects the lives of virtually everybody on earth whether they realise it or not. That means that IR is now more than ever a universal academic subject. That also means that world politics at the end of the twentieth century must accommodate a range and variety of states which are far more diverse—in terms of their cultures, religions, languages, ideologies, forms of government, military capacity, technological sophistication, levels of economic development, etc.—than ever before. That is a fundamental change in the state system and a fundamental challenge for IR scholars to under stand.

Contemporary World and International Relations

Many important questions in the study of international relations are connected with the theory and practice of sovereign statehood which, as indicated, is the central historical institution of world politics. But there are other important issues as well. That has led to ongoing debates about the proper scope of international relations. At one extreme the scholarly focus is exclusively on states and interstate relations; but at another extreme international relations includes almost everything that has to do with human relations across the world. It is important to study these different perspectives if we hope to have a balanced and rounded knowledge of IR.

Our reason for linking the various IR theories to states and the state system is to acknowledge the historical centrality of that subject. Even theorists who seek to get beyond the state usually take it as a starting-point : the state system is the main point of reference both for traditional and for new approaches. Later chapters will explore how each tradition of IR scholarship has attempted to come to grips with the sovereign state. There are debates about how we should conceptualise the state and different IR theories take somewhat different approaches. In later chapters we shall present contemporary debates on the future of the state. Whether its central importance in world politics may now be changing is a very important question in contemporary international relations scholarship. But the fact is that states and the state system remain at the center of academic analysis and discussion in international relations.

We must of course be alert to the fact that the sovereign state is a contested theoretical concept. When we ask the questions 'what is the state?' and 'what is the state system?' there will be different answers depending on the theoretical approach adopted: the realist answer will be different from the liberal answer, and those answers will be different from the International Society answer and from the answer given by IPE theories. None of these answers are strictly speaking either correct or incorrect because the truth is: the state is a multifaceted and somewhat confusing entity. The state system consequently is not an easy subject to understand, and it can be understood in different ways and with different points of emphasis. But there are ways of simplifying. It is helpful to think of the state as having two different dimensions, each divided into two broad categories. The first dimension is the state as a government versus the state as a country. Viewed from within, the state is the national government: it is the highest governing authority in a country: it possesses internal sovereignty. That is the *internal* aspect of the state. Main questions in relation to the internal aspect concern *state-society* relations; how the government rules the domestic society, the means of its power and the sources of its legitimacy, how it deals with the demands and concerns of individuals and groups which compose that domestic society, how it manages the national economy, what its domestic policies are, and so forth.

Viewed internationally, however, the state is not merely

a government: it is a populated territory with a national government and a society. In other words, it is a country. From that angle, both the government and the domestic society make up the state. If a country is a sovereign state it will be generally recognised as politically independent. That is the external aspect of the state in which the main questions concern *interstate* relations; how the governments and societies of state relate to each other and deal with each other, what the basis of those *interstate* relations are, what the foreign policies of particular states are, what the international organisations of the states are, how people from different states interact with each other and engage in transactions with each other, and so forth.

That brings us to the second dimension of the state, which divides the external aspect of sovereign statehood into two broad categories. The first category is the state viewed as a formal or legal institution in its relation with other states. That is the state as an entity which is recognised as sovereign or independent, enjoys membership in international organisations, and possesses various international rights and responsibilities. We shall refer to that first category as *juridical statehood*. Recognition is an essential element of juridical statehood. Recognition qualifies states for membership of International Society, including membership of the United Nations.

The absence of recognition denies it. Not every country is recognised as independent: as example is Quebec, which is a province of Canada. To become independent it must be recognised as such by existing sovereign states, by far the most important of which for Quebec are first Canada and second the United States. The countries that are recognised as sovereign states are always fewer than the countries that are not recognised but conceivably could be recognised. That is because independence is generally regarded as politically valuable. But the countries that are recognised as sovereign states usually have no desire to see new countries recognised because it would involve partition: existing states would lose territory, population, resources, power, status, etc. If partition became an accepted practice it would undermine international stability. Partition would set a dangerous precedent that could destablise the state system if a growing number of currently subordinated but potentially independent countries lined up to demand recognition as sovereign states. So, there may always be somebody knocking on the door of state sovereignty, but there is a great reluctance to open the door and let them in. That would be disruptive of the present state system—especially now that there are no more colonies and the entire inhabited territory of the world is enclosed within one global state system. So juridical statehood is carefully rationed by existing sovereign states. The second category is the state viewed as a substantial political-economic organisation.

That category has to do with the extent to which states have developed efficient political institutions, a solid economic basis, and a substantial degree of national unity, that is, of popular unity and support for the state. We shall refer to that second category as *empirical statehood*. Some states are very strong in the sense that they have a high level of empirical statehood. Most states in the West are like that. Many of those states are small, for example Sweden, Holland, and Luxemburg. A strong state in the sense of a high level of empirical statehood should be held separate from the notion of a strong power in the military sense. Some strong states are not militarily powerful; Denmark is an example. Some powers in the military sense, such as Russia, are not strong states. Canada is the unusual case of a highly developed country with an effective democratic government but with a major weakness in its statehood: the threat of Quebec to secede.

One of the most important conditions that throws

light on the existence of so many quasi-states in the Third World is that of economic underdevelopment. Their poverty and consequent shortages of investment, infrastructure (roads, schools, hospitals, etc.), modern technology, trained and educated people, and other socioeconomic assets or resources are among the most important factors that help us to understand why these states are so weak. The government and its institutions in these countries demonstrate little in the way of a solid foundation. The weakness of these states is a mirror of their poverty and technological backwardness, and as long as those conditions persist their incapacity as states is likely to persist as well. That profoundly affects the nature of the state system and also, therefore, the character of our IR theories.

Different conclusions can be drawn from the fact that empirical statehood varies so widely in the contemporary state system, from economically and technologically advanced and mostly Western states at one extreme to economically and technologically backward and mostly non-Western states at the other. Realist IR scholars focus mainly on the states at the centre of the system: the major powers and especially the great powers. They see Third World states as marginal players in a system of power politics that has always rested on the 'inequality of nations' (tucker 1977). Such marginal or peripheral states do not affect the system in any very significant way. Other IR scholars, usually liberals and International Society theorists, see the adverse conditions of quasi-states as a fundamental problem for the state system which raises issues not only of international order but also of international freedom and justice.

Some IPE scholars, usually Marxists, make underdevelopment of peripheral countries and the unequal relations between the centre and the periphery of the global economy the crucial explanatory element of their theory of the modern international system (wallerstein 1974). They investigate international linkages between the poverty of the Third

World, or the South, and the enrichment of America, Europe, and other parts of the North. They see the international economy as one overall "world system', with the developed capitalist states at the centre advancing at the expene of the weak, underdeveloped states at the periphery. According to these scholars, legal equality and political independence—what we have designated as 'juridical statehood'—is scarcely more than a polite façade that merely obscures the extreme vulnerability of poor Third World states and their domination and exploitation by the rich capitalist states of the West.

The underdeveloped countries certainly disclose in a striking way the profound empirical inequalities of contemporary would politics. But it is their possession of juridical statehood which reflects their membership of the state system that places that issue in sharp perspective, for it highlights the fact that the populations of some states—the developed countries—enjoy far better living conditions in virtually every respect than the populations of other states—the underdeveloped countries. The fact that underdeveloped countries belong to the same global state system as developed countries raises different questions than if they belonged to entirely separate systems, which was the case before the global state system was created. We can see the issues of security, freedom and progress, order and justice, and wealth and poverty far more clearly when it involves members of the same international system. For *inside* a system the same general standards and expectations apply. So if some states cannot meet common standards or expectations because of their underdevelopment, that becomes an international problem and not only a domestic problem or somebody else's problem. That is a major change from the past when most non-Western political systems either were outside the state system and operated according to different standards or they were colonies of Western imperial powers who were responsible for them as a matter of domestic policy rather than foreign policy.

These developments are a reminder that the world of states is a dynamic, changing world and not a static, unchanging one. In international relations, as in other spheres of human relations, nothing stands still for very long. International relations change alongwith everything else: politics, economics, science, technology, education, culture, and the rest. An obvious case in point is technological innovation, which has profoundly shaped international relations from the beginning and continues to shape it in significant ways that are never entirely predictable. Over the centuries new or improved military technology has had a profound impact on the balance of power, arms races, imperialism and colonialism, military alliances, the nature of war, and much else. Economic growth has permitted greater wealth to be devoted to military budgets, and has provided a foundation for the development of larger, better-equipped, and more effective military forces. Scientific discoveries have made possible new technologies, such as transportation or information technologies, which have had the effect of knitting the world more closely together and making national borders more permeable. Literacy, mass education, and expanded higher education have enabled governments to increase the capacity of their state and expand their activities into more and more specialised spheres of society and economy.

It cuts both ways, of course, because highly educated people do not like being told what to think or what to do. Changing cultural values and ideas have affected not only the foreign policy of particular states but also the shape and direction of international relations. For example, the ideologies of anti-racism and anti-imperialism that were first articulated by intellectuals in Western countries eventually undermined Western overseas empires in Asia and Africa, and helped bring about the decolonisation process by making the moral justification of colonialism increasingly difficult and eventually impossible.

The examples of the impact of social change on international relations are almost endless in their number and variety. However, this should suffice to make the point that social change affects states and the state system. The relationship is undoubtedly reversible; the state system also has an impact on politics, economics, science, technology, education, culture, and the rest. For example, it has been compellingly argued that it was the development of a state system in Europe that was decisive in propelling that continent ahead of all other continents during the modern era. The competition of the independent European states within their state system—their military competition, their economic competition, their scientific and technological competition—catapulted those states ahead of non-European political systems which were not spurred by the same degree of competition. One scholar has made the point as follows: "The states of Europe...were surrounded by actual or potential competitors. If the government of one were lax, it impaired its own prestige and military security...The state system was an insurance against economic and technological stagnation. We should not conclude, therefore, that the state system merely reacts to change; it is also a cause of change.

The fact of social change raises a more fundamental question. At some point should we expect states to change so much that they are no longer states in the sense discussed here? For example, if the process of economic globalisation continues and makes the world one single market-place and one single production site, will the state system then be obsolete? We have in mind the following activities which might bypass states: ever increasing international trade and investment, expanding multinational business activity, enlarged NGO (non-governmental organisation) activities, increasing regional and global communications, the growth of the Internet, expanding and ever extending trans-portation networks, exploding travel and tourism, massive human migration, cumulative environmental pollution, expanded regional integration, the growth of trading communities the global expansion of science and technology, continuous downsising of government, increased privatisation and other activities which have the effect of increasing interdependence across borders.

Or will sovereign states and the state system find ways of adapting to those social charges, just as they have adapted time and again to other major changes during the past 350 years? Some of those changes were just as fundamental; the scientific revolution of the seventeenth century, the enlightenment of the eighteenth century, the encounter of Western and non-Western civilisations over the course of several centuries, the growth of Western imperialism and colonialism, the Industrial Revolution of the eighteenth and nineteenth centuries the rise and spread of nationalism in the nineteenth and twentieth centuries, the revolution of anti-colonialism and decolonisation in the twentieth century, the spread of mass public education, the growth of the welfare state, and much else.

The state system is a historical institution fashioned by people. The population of the world have not always lived in sovereign states. For most of recorded human history people have lived under different kinds of political organisation. In medieval times, political authority was chaotic and dispersed. Most people were dependent on a large number of different authorities—some of them political, some religious—with diverse responsibilities and power, from the local ruler and landlord to the King in a distant capital city, from parish priest to the Pope in far away Rome. In the modern state, authority is centralised in one legally supreme government, and people live under the standard laws of that government. The development of the modern state went a long way towards organising political authority and power along rational and national lines.

The state system was a European state system in the first instance. During the era of Western imperialism the rest of the world was dominated by Europeans, both politically and economically. Only with Asian and African decolonisation, after the Second World War, did the state system become a global institution. The globalisation of the state system vastly increased the variety of its member states and consequently its diversity. The most important difference is between strong states with a high level of empirical statehood and weak quasi-states, which have formal sovereignty but very little substantial statehood. In other words, decolonisation contributed to a huge and deep internal division in the state system between the rich North and the poor South: i.e., between developed countries at the centre, which dominate the system politically and economically, and underdeveloped countries at the peripheries, which have limited political and economic influence. People often expect states to uphold certain key values: security, freedom, order, justice, and welfare. IR theory concerns the ways in which states do or do not ensure those values. Historically the system of states consists of many heavily armed states, including a small number of great powers which often have been military rivals and sometimes have gone to war with each other. That reality of the state as a war machine underlines the value of security.

2

India's Peace Initiatives

India's efforts for peaceful co-existence got a concrete shape with the five principles formulated on 29 April, 1954 as a part of the agreement between India and China. These five principles came to be known as Panchsheel, though the conflict between India and China in 1962 may raise questions about the validity of the panchsheel, its five principles still hold good. These are:

- Mutual respect for each other's territorial integrity and sovereignty.
- Mutual non-aggression.
- Mutual non-interference in each other's internal affairs.
- Equality and mutual benefit.
- Peaceful co-existence.

These five principles were also adopted by the First Afro-Asian Conference at bandung in the year 1955. These five principles have in fact, played a very significant role in India's foreign policy.

India's Policy of Non-alignment

While developing its foreign policy, India has taken into account two major considerations. One for the national interest, and the other for global concerns like peace, human rights and justice to all, co-existence and world economic development. After the Second World War, the world was getting divided into two opposite blocs. One bloc was headed by the U.S.A. and the other by the former Soviet Union. This was the time when, as a follow-up of the decolonisation process in the entire world, new independent countries were emerging. These new independent countries were joining either of the two blocs. In a situation like this, India, herself a newly independent country, rightly felt that a division of the world into two blocs will be harmful not only to India but to world peace and development also. The Government of India decided not to align itself to any of the power blocs. It declared it s foreign policy as a policy of non-alignment. Non-alignment primarily means a policy of not belonging to any bloc. Non-alignment, however, does not mean that India will remain neutral and not take any position on important world problems. It simply means that IDIA is not obliged to take the side of any of the big powers it can take independent position on international issues. India can follow her foreign policy independently. In her effort to pursue the policy of non-alignment, two other countries, Yugoslavia and Egypt came forward and joined India.

In fact, India's fruitful contribution to the achievement of international peace and cooperation has been possible because of its independent foreign policy. In the fifties, non-alignment as a policy was adopted by a small number of countries, but by the nineties it had become a very big movement. The formation and expansion of Non-aligned Movement has been directly connected with the emergence and growth of the decolonisation process in the world.

Although the era of cold war is over and with the disintegration of Soviet Union, the two blocs do not exist, NAM is a definite force in the present day world; it has not become irrelevant. NAM is a free and equal association of States united by common interests to pursue independent foreign policy, NAM remains the largest political formation in the world, next only to the UN. India's endeavour to promote international peace and cooperation through its foreign Policy and through NAM is noteworthy. Besides the problems of security and understanding between nations, India keeps its eyes open towards important social and economic issues which have international repercussions. In the shrinking world of today, every country gets affected by the happenings in other countries.

India's Peace Efforts in the Sub-continent

India's sincere efforts in maintaining peace in the sub-continent have been reflected several times through its relations with neighbouring countries. In this regard, a special mention of the India-Pakistan Declarations from time to time highlighting peace and understanding between the two countries needs to be mentioned into. Signing of he famous Tashkent Declaration of 1966 is one such example. Through this declaration, both the countries affirmed the need for negotiated settlement of disputes.

In 1972, the Simla Agreement was another effort of settling disputes between India and Pakistan in a peaceful manner. In the year 1999, India's prime Minister accompanied by some noted Indians visited Pakistan as a goodwill gesture which came to be know as 'Bus Diplomacy'. This was another effort on India's part to maintain an environment of peace and understanding. In 2001, Pakistan's President and his delegates visited India and had a meeting with the Indian delegation headed by the Prime Minister of India. This meetings known, 'Agra Summit'. But all thee initiatives failed to bring lasting peace between the two countries. India's endeavour has always been to maintain peaceful relations with her neighbours and other countries of the world. After the inhuman attacks by terrorists in the U.S.A. on 11 September, 2001, Indian lost no time in denouncing the attack in strongest terms and offered to extend all help to the people and the government of the USA. Yet, again India faced a similar attack on its Parliament on 13 December 2001. All the terrorists were overpowered and killed in the encounter. As a member of the South Asian Association for regional Cooperation (SAARC), India has embarked on a programme of comprehensive economic cooperation through the dynamic South Asian countries.

United Nations

United Nations was formed after the end of the Second World War. The horrors of the war terrified the entire humanity. With the noble objective of saving the world from the scourge of another war. United Nations was founded on 24 October, 1945. Originally fifty-one nations became members of the UN. Over the years, the membership of UN has grown. At present, United Nations has more than 191 members. The main cause of increase in membership is the decolonization of many Asian and African countries. Like other organisations, UN also has a Charter. It sets down the main objectives of the UN. It also lays down the structure of the UN and the functions of its various organs.

The headquarter of the United Nations is situated in New York city of U.S.A. the UN has six main organs. These are the General Assembly, the Security Council, the Trusteeship council, Economic and Social Council, the International Court of Justice and the Secretariat.

All member states of the UN are members of the General Assembly. Each member has one vote in the General Assembly. It is the general policy-making body of the UN.

The Security Council is the most effective organ and carries out the task of maintaining international peace. It has 15 members. The U.S.A. Russia, Britain, France and China are its permanent members. These five members have special power known as veto power. On all issues, it is necessary to secure support of all these five members. If any member uses its veto, no decision can be taken on that issue. Trusteeship Council monitors and supervises the administration of trust territories. In order to solve disputes, International Court of Justice is there in the UN system. The UN has a Secretary General who functions with the assistance of a large Secretariat. The Secretary General plays a very important role in solving international problems.

In the preceding paragraphs we have read about the formation of the United Nations, its objective and its structure. Now we are going to read about India's role in the functioning of the UN. From the very beginning, India's foreign policy recognized the necessity and importance of a world body like the UN to maintain peace, understanding and cooperation in the world. The Constitution of India through the Directive Principles of State Policy directs the government to promote international peace and seek peaceful settlement of international disputes. India has been playing a significant role in promoting world peace through the United Nations. India has always expressed faith in the aims and objectives of the UN. Whenever the United Nations force was set up for peace-keeping, India offered her services. Indian troops have taken part in some of the most difficult operations. Indian armed forces helped in the maintenance of peace in Korea, Egypt, and Congo. In fact, India has taken part in the UN peace-keeping operations in different countries. Its most significant contribution has been in Africa and Asia. Besides Korea, Egypt and Congo, Indian army provided an Observer Mission in Yemen in 1996. India also participated in the UN operations in Cyprus. The UN had set up a Observer Group to monitor the situation on Ira-Iraq border, where

India also participated. In UN's operation in Nambia, the Force Commdander was an Indian Army officer. India has risked the lives of its soldiers in peace-keeping efforts in a large number of operations. In every operation, Indian soldiers have proved their professional excellence.

India's Role in the U.N.O.

India is the founding member of the United Nations Organisation which has played a significant role in maintaining world peace efforts and promoting international co-operation. India, as its responsible member, has worked for the betterment of humanity as a whole even beyond her frontiers. India was among the first countries to support the admission of Communist China to the U.N.O. though it was opposed by a big power like the U.S.A. India realized that a large chunk of the Humanity could not be left out of this world organisation. In the past, there arose several localized conflicts world over which threatened world peace The U.N. played the role of a peace keeper and was called upon to restore peace. India always supported U.N.'s peace efforts. T was in the forefront in sending her troops and equipments as a part of the U.N. peace Keeping force to the affected areas. Whether it was war torn Rwanda or famine stricken Somalia, Indian peace keepers did commendable services to mitigate the sufferings of the people of these wretched countries. It won appreciation for his work from all the nations of the world.

India has always opposed imperialism and colonialism. It persistently championed the cause of people suffering under colonial rule in Asia, Africa and elsewhere in the world. We supported the freedom movements in African countries like Ghana, Kenya, Togoland, Morocco, Tunisia, Algeria Sough Africa etc. We also supported Indonesia in her struggle against the domination of Holland. We strongly protested against the U.S. imperialism in Vietnam and

French imperialism in Indo-China. We condemned the Russian aggression in Hungary, of France in Algeria and the British in Cyprus.

An important principle of our plicy towards other nations was oppositionto racial discrimination. Our national leadershave always opposed discrimination on the bsis of race and colour. We severely opposed the maltreatment of Black people bythe Whites in South Africa. We gave full support to the U.N. Resolution against the policy of discrimination followed by the Government of South Africa. Indian protested against the American policy towards the Blacks in their countries. India gave full support to Nelso Mandela, a great freedom fighter of South Africa. In April 1994, Mandela succeeded in his mission and became the first on-white President of his country. India has thus done commendable service to the humanity by opposing racism and racial discrimination.

Non-Alignment

India played a significant role in the organization of the Non-Alignment movement which has helped to formulate world opinion. At the peak of the cold war years, when the world was hopelessly divided into hostile camps, India took the initiative in the formation of the Non-Aligned Movement. It was a lone voice which unified the developing third World countries into a neutral bloc and thus steering them clear of the two warring camps. In fact, the NAM was the culmination of the efforts of India's Prime Minister Jawahar Lal Nehru, Gamal Abdul Nassar of Egypt and Marshal Tito of Yugoslavia in the formation of a neutral front. There is no doubt that Non-Aligned Movement has a moderating effect on the world politics.

India plays the role of having a soothing effect on the world politics. India has given the message of co-existence through its principles of Panchsheel or Indira Gandhi's

"Fair, Firm and Friendly" regard for the seething mankind. The five principles of Panchsheel are

(a) Mutual respect for the territorial integrity and sovereignty of all the countries

(b) Mutual non-aggression

(c) Non-interference in the internal affairs of any countries

(d) To work for mutual equality and benefit Peaceful co-existence or Live and Let Live.

These principles promote international peace and security these principles were accepted by many Afro-Asian countries. India has declared in clear terms that it is not going to use atomic energy for making atom bombs. It has time and again called upon the rich nations of the world to destroy their nuclear weapons and work for international peace. India believes in the use of atomic energy for peaceful purposes such as generation of electric power and in the field of medicine.

Peace Initiative and other Countries

Other countries of the world took initiative sin case there was danger of war or disturbances in any part of the world. Russia has several times shown its concern at the piling of farms by other countries. It has always supported the plans for disarmaments. During the Vietnam War, most countries of Africa and Asia condemned U.S. involvement in this war. Japan has remained the champion of peace in the world after the Second World War. All the member countries of the Non-Aligned Movement have supported the efforts of the U.N.O. when peace was disturbed in any region of the world.

3

Motives of Colonialism and Imperialism

India's own bitter experiences of suffering, exploitation, discrimination and its own long fight against colonialism made it committed to fight against colonialism in all forms. Consequently, India advocated the cause of dependent and exploited nations of Asia and Africa in various bodies of the UN. On India's initiative, the UN passed a resolution on 14 December, 1960 called the "Declaration on the grating of independence to colonial countries and peoples". For the implementation of this declaration, India was appointed a member of the special committee. India firmly supported the freedom movements in Asia and Africa. It consistently championed the cause of the exploited nations against the colonial powers. The UN which used to be dominated the by the western countries, especially by the United States and the Europeans, came under the influence of the newly liberated countries, popularly called Third World or Non-aligned countries. The newly independent Afro-Asian countries, worked as a group in the UN to assert their views. India stands for the solidarity among the newly liberated Afro-Asian countries. In this situation, the western powers or the former colonial states or developed nations find themselves challenged. Now, the difference of opinion in the General Assembly deliberations over the issue of freedom and development between the developed and developing nations is clearly marked. With the joining of new states, especially newly liberated ones, and with the disintegration of the USSR the present strength the of the UN has reached 191.

However, colonialism is definitely more subtle than imperialism, since it involves a deeper and more extensive penetration in the life of the native people of the colonies. It involves social, economic, political and cultural control of the people of the colonial power over the people of the colonies. Imperialism is relatively more formal in nature and involves, basically, a system of political rule over the imperialised state.

Meaning of Colonialism

Colonialism as European Colonialism E.M. Winslow observes, "Colonialism is the occupation of virgin territory in which conflict was incidental, or even unnecessary, and subordinate to the desire of Europeans to find new place to live." J.A. Hobson offers a simple, lucid and comprehensive definition of colonialism. According to him, "colonialism is a natural over flow of nationality, its test is the power of the colonists to transplant the civilisation they represent to the new natural and social environment is which they find themselves. Colonialism as such implies the migration of nationals from their home to territories abroad for permanently settling in these territories. It involves the domination of life and culture of the ecolonised people by the population of the colonist state.

The main features of colonialism include:

- Domination of an alien minority by asserting

racial and cultural superiority over a materially inferior native majority.

- Contact between a machine oriented, better developed, economically powerful civilisation with a backward, underdeveloped, poor civilisation, and
- The imposition of the superior and better developed civilisation over the weaker and poorer civilisation. The colonialisation of African people by the Portuguese. British, French and Belgians from 15 century to late 19th century, offers the classical example of colonialism in international politics. It has been a source of bestial exploitation and extermination of the indigenous way of the life, resources and culture of the African people.

Imperialism vs. Colonialism

The past victims of Imperialism or Colonialism, both these systems are identical in so far both involve foreign rule, economic exploitation of their land and resources and cultural subordiantion to the aliens. In the theory of international politics, the systems of imperialism and colonialism are intimately related but are different systems.

The main points of difference between the two are as under:

(a) Colonialsm is comparatively older than Imperialism.

(b) Imperialism is basically a system of political control—foreign rule over other territories. Colonialism on the other hand involves a domination of the life and culture of the colonised people by the people of the colonist state.

(c) Since imperialism involves the imposition of alien rule over other people, it necessarily involves the use of military power and war. As against this,

Colonialism does not necessarily involve the use of force as it can be affected by the natural flow of nationality to virgin territories and backward countries.

(d) Colonialism as a system of control is more subtle and less formal than Imperialism. Imperialism is more rigid and autocratic in approach.

While comparing, "Imperialism and Colonialism, E.M. Winslow observes, "Imperialism is something more organised, more militant, more self-consciously aggressive and bent on objectives, above and beyond those of colonialism."

Townsend and Peake regard Colonialism as "a particular kind of imperialism." These distinctions between imperialism and Colonialism are true only in theory. In actual practice both are highly exploitive and destructive of life, economy and culture of the people of colonies, and imperialised states. In imperialism, political control and rule is more rigid and extensive than colonialism. In colonialism, the stress is upon the economic and cultural domination over the people of the colonies.

Presently both imperialism and colonialism have got transferred into new-imperialism and new-colonialism. Neo—colonialism is the popular term to designate both new imperialism and new-colonialism. The era of imperialism and colonialism is now over but the era of neo-colonialism has emerged. In this era, the people of former colonies and empires have been in a position to secure political freedom from the yoke of imperialism and colonialism, but at the same time they continue to be economically dependent upon their former colonial and imperial masters. Classical colonialism and imperialism have come to be replaced by neo-colonalism—a system in which politically independent, newly emerged sovereign states continue to be economically dominated by the rich states most of which are the old imperial and colonial powers. The need to fight neo-colonialism continues to be the biggest need and the most serious challenge of the contemporary international relations. Imperialism was used by them as an effective means for expanding their power beyond their own territories. They justified it as a moral and legitimate instrument and used it for securing the goals of national interests as well as for promoting 'the welfare of the backward people.'

Most of the imperial powers mostly the European nations justified their imperialist policies as policies designed to uplift, civilise and christianise the backward people of Asia and Africa. They justified their policy as means to discharge 'White Man's Eurden', *i.e.,* to secure the uplift of backward and none-white peoples of the world. Maintenance and expansion of imperial and colonial empires was considered to be the basic aim of their foreign policies. Such practices continued to be followed almost till the middle of the 20th century. However, in the middle of the 20th century imperialism and colonialism became the objects of strong condemnation and repudiation. Even the formerly imperial and colonial powers now became eager to demonstrate their opposition to these 'evils.'

The victims of imperialism and colonialism became the staunchest critics and opponents of these 'evils' and one by one they became successful in attaining their independence from the yoke of Imperialism and Colonialism. As independent sovereign states they became totally committed to wipe out completely these evils and the new form of these evils—neo-colonialism. Anti-Imperialism or Anti-colonialism became the strongest movement of our times.

Meaning of Imperialism

The term 'imperialism' means the practice of extending the power, control or rule by a country over the political and economic life of areas outside its own borders. This may be does through military or other means, and particularly through 'colonialism' or the practice of acquiring colonies by conquest or other means and making them dependent. I may be remembered that occupation of or direct rule over a country or people by another country is not always an essential feature of imperialism. The essential feature of the relations between an imperialist country and the country over which it has established its control or the colony which it has acquired, is exploitation, with or without direct political control. This means that the imperialist country and the country over which it has established its control or the colony which it has acquired, is exploitation, which or without direct political control. This means that the imperialist country, or metropolis (literal meaning 'mother country'), as it is sometimes called, subordinates the colony or the country which the metropolis indirectly controls to serve its own economic and political interests. Most countries of Asia, including India, and Africa, and many other parts of the world were until recent years under the control of one imperialist country or an other. These included countries which were not directly ruled by the imperialist countries but were exploited by them more or less in the same way as countries over which direct imperialist rule had been established. In the present-day world, when almost all countries of the world are politically independent, imperialist control over other countries has not come to an end. The practice of exploitation, particularly economic exploitation and domination of independent but economically less developed countries, is often called neo-colonialism.'

Almost all nations use it to criticise the policies and actions of their opponents. America used to critical the former Soviet Union as an imperial power attempting to imperialise other nations under the cloak of communism. The later used to criticize the former as an imperialist country working for expanding capitalistic imperialism over other countries of the world. China was always critical of both America as a bourgeoise capitalist-imperialist country and the USSR as a social-imperialist country. India has been critical of China as a country pursuing an imperialist policy of territorial expansionism. Pakistan always criticises India as country having an imperialist design in south-Asia. In fact, as *Raymond Buell* observes," Every unjustifiable demand made by one government upon another—every aggressive war—is called *imperialistic*. Imperialism is a word which covers many a sin." It is a commonly used term for criticising the policies of the opponents and this makes it difficult for us to precisely answer the question: what is imperialism?

Highlighting the difficulty faced in defining imperialism, *Palmer and Perkins* have observed, "Imperialism can be discussed, denounced, defended, and died for, but it cannot be defined in any generally acceptable way. It means different things to different people." The following definitions of imperialism as given by various scholars illustrate the truth of the observations made by Palmer and Perkins.

(a) According to *Charles A. Beard* "imperialism is the employment of the engines of government diplomacy to acquire territories, protectorates, and/or spheres of influence occupied usually by other races or peoples, and to promote industrial, trade, and investment opportunities."

(b) Parker T. Moon defines it as "Domination of Non-European native races by totally dissimilar European nations."

(c) According to *Prof. Schuman*, "Imperialism is the imposition by force and violence of alien rule upon subject people, despite all moralising and pretensions to the contrary."

(d) *Schumpeter* defines it as an "atavistic force, ancient in inception, decadent and self-conscious in an age of rationalism yet still powerful enough to lord it over its rival, the upstart capitalism."

(e) *Moritz Julius Bonn* observes, "imperialism is a policy which aims at creating, organising, maintaining an empire: that is, a state of vast size composed of various more or less district national units and subject to a single centralized will."

(f) In the words of *C.D. Berns,* "Imperialism is the name of a common law and order system for different nations and races."

(g) *N.L. Bukharin* defines imperialism as, "the attempt to conquer other countries."

Discussing these definition, Palmer and Perkins opine that it is very difficult to offer a single acceptable definition of imperialism. They, therefore, adopt a different way for explaining imperialism. They specify the following characteristics of imperialism:

(i) Imperialism is a highly subjective term, the writers define it pretty as much as they please.

(ii) Imperialism has become more of an epithet than anything else. The communists use it to stigmatise the policies of the western state and the western powers use it to criticize and reject communist policies.

(iii) There are four common points in the various definitions of imperialism:

(a) Imperialism may or may not have non-economic motivations;

(b) It may pertain to a very limited operation—a "vast empire" need not be contemplated at all;

(c) It need not involve a difference of race—"there

may very well be imperialism within a single race"; and

(d) It may be planned or unplanned.

(iv) Imperialism may or may not involve a high regard for the welfare of the inhabitants of the imperialised colonies. It may be developmental or exploitative.

(v) It may be economically profitable for the imperialist country or it may be decidedly unprofitable.

Palmer and Perkins give their own definition of imperialism as, "A relationship in which one area and its people are subordinate to another area a and its government... Imperialism in essence always involves subordination; it is a power relationship without moral implications of any kind."

Morgenthau's Explanation of Imperialism. In defining imperialism, Morgenthau adopts a method of elimination. Before defining imperialism, he clarifies what imperialism is not.

What Imperialism is Not. Morgenthau holds that three types of policies cannot be called imperialistic and as such while defining imperialism we should refrain from using the principles of these three policies:

Imperialism is Expansionism. It aims at the overthrow of status quo. In the first instance, Morgenthau holds, "Not every foreign policy aiming at an increase in the power of a nation is necessarily a manifestation of imperialism." All the nations attempting to increase their national powers cannot be called imperialists because imperialism involves expansionism. 'Imperialism' and 'increase in power' are not synonymous. Imperialism is a policy that aims at the overthrow of status quo, at a reversal of the power relations between two or more nations." A policy seeking increase of power through adjustment, leaving the power relations intact, is not imperialistic because it works within the general framework of status quo.

Imperialism is not a static policy of preservation. Secondly, Morgenthau observes, "Not every foreign policy aiming at the preservation of an empire that already exists is imperialism." Very often imperialism is wrongly identified with the policy of maintaining an existing empire or the predominant position in power relations. Actually imperialism should not be equated with static conservatism. Imperialism has a dynamic connotation—to increase power beyond the territory of the nation.

It is different from the policy of status quo. It involves increase in national power and not the maintenance of national power. "A foreign policy which seeks to maintain and preserve the status quo cannot be called imperialistic; the foreign policy that seeks to change the status quo alone can be called imperialistic" Churchill's policy of maintaining the British empire was a policy of status quo and not of imperialism. To quote *Morgenthau,* "When Churchill refused in 1942 'to preside over the liquidation of the British empire,' he was speaking not as an imperialist but as a conservative in foreign affairs, a defender of the status quo of empire."

Imperialism is not an Economic Instrument. Thirdly Morgenthau refuses to accept imperialism as an economic instrument of policy. He holds that though economic gain can be one of the motives of imperialism, it cannot be and it is never the basis or the core of imperialism. Imperialism is a political device which aims at the extension of national power beyond the territories of the nation following the policy of imperialism. After having explained what imperialism is not, *Morgenthau* defines imperialism as "the expansion of state power beyond its borders, for economic gains, territorial acquisitions and governance of different races."

According to Morgenthau there are three factors which lead to imperialism in international relations:

- First, the peace treaties that are made after a war and which create a new power structure in international relations lead to imperialism. For example the Treaty of Versailles was the source of imperialist policies of Hitler and Mussolini.
- Secondly, the attempts made by some nations to keep other nations in a state of permanent subordination also lead to imperialism.
- Finally, the existence of weak states in international system impells the powerful states towards the pursuance of a policy of imperialism towards them.

All these three factors create conditions which favour the formulation and implementation of imperialist policies.

On the basis of these definitions of imperialism, we can say that imperialism is a policy of subjugating other countries for the purposes of territorial expansionism, expansion of political power, exploitation of their economic resources and for establishing cultural domination over the people of imperialised countries. Charles Hodges has offered a comprehensive definition, which can be adopted as it generally correct definition of imperialism. He observes" Imperialism is a projection externally, directly or indirectly, of the alien political, economic, or cultural power of one nation into the internal life of another people...it involves the imposition of control, open or covert, direct or indirect— of one people by another.

Motives and Goals

Both are highly exploitive mechanisms which aim at the complete domination and ultimate extermination of the indigenous social and cultural systems of the people of colonies and imperialised states. Imperialism and Colonialism are closely related concepts with almost totally similar motives and goals. Both involve the imposition of an allien rule and culture over the native people. The difference between the two is made only in theory only, in practice both are equally dangerous and harmful systems. Their basis, despite all noble pretensions, is always immoral and selfish interests of the people of colonist and imperial powers.

Motives and policies

Because of the similarities between the two, we can be justified in discussing under one heading the motives, goals of Imperialism and Colonialism. The policy of imperialism that a nation adopts is motivated by a number of possible gains that the nation can secure through its rule over other states. It is designed to serve several interests of imperial power. The following factors usually provide strong motivation to imperialism:

Economic Gains, one of the primary objectives of Imperialism is to secure economic gains by utilising, rather exploiting, the raw material potential of the subject nation. The search for markets for getting vital raw materials, the need to find markets for selling the goods and the quest for new fields of investment of surplus capital, provide strong motives for the pursuance of an imperialist policy.

In the words of Dr. Heinrich Schnee, "Greet industrial nations need colonies to supply them with raw materials." "The fight for raw materials," observes Dr. Shacht, "plays the most important part in world politics..." The need to secure raw materials for their industries has been indeed a major reason which has encouraged the developed and rich nations to pursue imperialism. Similarly, the possession of colonies, dependencies and territories always affords a big opportunity to sell the surplus goods. The imperial power seeks markets for selling the surplus goods produced by its industrial units. The markets of the colonies, because of chronic backwardness, constitute big consumer markets and hence attract the imperial powers. Further, and empire helps a powerful and rich nation to invest its surplus capital in the colonies. Surplus capital needs investment either at home or abroad. At home the opportunities are always limited and very often domestic investment reaches a saturation point beyond which investment becomes unprofitable. As against this investment abroad, particularly in colonies, offers big opportunities for highly profitable investments. This factor provides a strong motivation to imperialism.

Economic Movities

The economic motives of imperialism are so powerful that many scholars try to explain imperialism solely in terms of economic theories. They offer a number of economic theories of imperialism. Imperialism is, of course, not an economic instrument or policy, nevertheless, it cannot be denied that economic gains provide very strong motivation to the policy of imperialism.

Power and Prestige, to be more and more powerful and thus secure prestige in international relations has been a psychological motive behind the policy of imperialism in international relations. The lust for adventure, power, prestige and glory which seemed to accrue from a vast colonial empire not only to the governing classes but to the masses of the colonising nations, the new sentiment of pride and superiority which animated even the lowest members of the white races in their dealings with the 'backward' races have been powerful psychological motives of imperialism. The colonial possession is always considered as an addition to the national prestige of the imperialistic state. This ideal was stated by Mussolini when he said,

"The fascist state is a will to power and an empire. The Roman tradition is the idea of force. In the Fascist doctrine the imperial idea is not only a territorial, military and mercantile expansion but also one of spiritual and moral expansion." For fascism, "the tendency to the imperial ideal means expansion of the nation and is a manifestation of vitality." In a similar way it was the boast of Englishmen in which they glorified in saying that "the sun of the British Empire never sets." Thus the lust for power and prestige has always been a strong motive for imperialism.

White Man's Burden or Humanitarian Motive. The supporters of imperialism advocate that it is motivated by the humanitarian motive of uplifting the poor and backward people—the non-white peoples. It is projected, as Kiplin described, as the white man's burden to help the development of others. Such a notion is based on the view that the white race is a superior race and it is its prime duty to uplift the inferior races. Supporters of such a motive believe in abolishing ignorance, slavery and cannibalism from amongst the backward people and to civilise them by imparting to them their own religion and civilisation. This aspect of imperialism was well-expressed by President Mckinley, who while giving reason for annexing the Phillippine Islands declared, "there was nothing left for us to do but to take them all, and to educate the Phillipinese and uplift and civilise and christianise them as our fellowmen for whom Christ also died." Joseph Chamberlain, the leading exponent of imperialism, too declared in 1893; "It is our duty to take our share in the work of civilisation in Africa." Humanitarian motive is rightly termed by P.T. Moon as "Aggressive altruism" because it means using brutal force to impose on unwilling native peoples the blessings of French or German or British or American civilization. Under it the "superior variety of European civilisation" was sought to be made operative in Africa and Asia.

Humanitarian motive is in fact used by the imperialists to cloak their egoistic selfishness with professed altruism. Psychological Satisfaction—Nationalism. Nationalism is one of the fundamental motives of Imperialism and colonialism. "Imperialism," observes Hans John, "Is for the most part a later phase in the process begun by nationalism. Nationalism strives to unite the members of the nation, politically and territorially, in a state organisation. When that is accomplished, the struggle for the possession of the earth proceeds further...Thus imperialism and nationalism are interlocked." In fact aggressive nationalism always leads to imperialism.

Securing of National Defence. The control over the men and material resources of the imperialised territories or colonies considerably strengthens the ability of the imperial power to defend itself in wars with other states. In the two world wars, Britain depended very heavily upon India for the supply of soldiers and vital resources for the defence of the British empire. In the 19th century, Britain used Afghanistan, Iran and Tibet as buffer states for the defence of India against Russia. The colonial resources greatly add to the strength of the imperial power. During First World War, France drew nearly 5,00,000 troops and 2,00,000 workers from her colonies.

In both the world wars Britain's successes largely due to its ability to exploit the man-power and other resources of the colonies which constituted the British empire. Adjustment of Surplus Population. One of the important motives of imperialism is to adjust its surplus population in overseas colonies and territories. Many nations, particularly Germany, Italy and Japan, justified their policy of colonial acquisitions on the basis of necessity of adjusting their surplus populations. Mussolini's Fascism openly advocated "Italy's surplus manpower must emigrate." Thus, the need to send surplus population abroad has been one of the motives of imperialism and colonialism. However, this motive has not effectively worked in practice. Between 1884-1914, Germany annexed a number of colonies, but it could lead to the settlement of a very small proportion of German population in these colonies. Similarly, the number of Italians who settled in Italy's African Empire was also insignificant. Japan too failed to settle the desired number of its people in Korea, Formosa and Manchuria, commenting upon these failures of the imperial powers to settle their populations abroad.

Palmer and Perkins have observed, "All imperialist states have failed completely to win as much enthusiasm for home as for flags in those far away places with strange-sounding names." Besides these six primary motives of imperialism, the desire to spread a particular religion, e.g., Christianity, in other parts of the globe, the need for maintaining a particular balance the power relations, the desire to spread a particular ideology and the desire to export ideological revolutions to other countries have also been the motives of imperialism.

Goals of Imperialism

Imperialism is born out of three particular conditions, viz.

(i) Peace treaties after war involving a new power structure,

(ii) the desire to maintain others permanently subordinate, and

(iii) the existence of weak states, there are, observes Morgenthau three goals of Imperialism. An imperial power wishes to have a local preponderance or a continental empire or a world empire. As such these three can be described as goals of imperialism.

Local Preponderance, an imperial power trying to extend its rule or control over the states around it, pursues local preponderance as the goal. Such a policy seeks to overthrow the status quo and to established preponderance within self-chosen limits. IT is a case of localised imperialism and the best examples are offered by the monarchical policies of the 18th and 19th centuries. In the eighteenth century, Frederick the Great, Louis XV, Maria Theresa, Peter the Great, and Gatherine II were the moving forces of this kind of foreign policy. In the 19th century, Bismarck was the master of this type of imperialistic policy. Bismarck's foreign policy was always guided by the goal of Germany's preponderance in central Europe.

The traditional objectives of Russian imperialism, such as control of Finland, Eastern Europe, the Balkans, the Dardanelles and Iran, were also of a localised nature. "The limits of this type of imperialism," write Morgenthau, "are not, as in the case of the geographically limited type, primarily a product of the objective facts of nature, beyond which it would be either technically difficult or politically unwise to go. On the contrary, they are primarily the result of a free choice among several alternatives, one of which might be a policy of the status quo, another continental imperialism, a third localised imperialism. In the 18th century the third alternative recommended itself because the existing concept of powers, each of about the same strength, discouraged any attempt at continental imperialism. The experience of Louis XVI showed how hazardous such an attempt could be. Further more, eighteenth century imperialism was motivated mainly by considerations of monarchical power and glory and not by the mass emotions of modern nationalism. These considerations operated within a common framework of monarchical traditions and European civilization which imposed upon the actors on the political scene a moral restraint." This led to the adoption of local preponderance as the goal of imperialism. The second possible goal of an imperialist policy can be the establishment of rule over the countries of a continent, that is to imperialise the continent by establishing superiority and control over the policies of all other countries of the continent. It can be called geographically determined imperialism. Louis XIV, Napolean III and William II were all motivated by the goals of continental imperialism.

The kingdom of Picdmont under Cavour seeking the domination of the Italian peninsula in 1850s, the different participants in the Balkans wars of 1912 and 1913, aspiring for high money in the Balkans, and Mussolini's attempt to make the Mediterranean an Italian lake, are the examples of geographically determined imperialism almost on a continental basis. The United States policy of gradual expansion of American power over North America was primarily determined by the geographical limits of a continent. The same type of imperialism constitutes the essence of American foreign policy towards Western Hemisphere as a whole.

The Monroe Doctrine was designed for securing a status quo for Western Hemisphere in the politics of non-American powers. It was erected as a protective shield behind which the United States could establish its predominance within that geographic region. American policy towards Latin America was again a policy of imperialism guided by the goal of a virtual continental empire of the United States. *World Empire.* When a nation following an imperialist policy is guided by the goal of conquering the whole world or at least to go in for unlimited imperialism, we can say that world empire is the goal of such an imperial policy. The outstanding examples of unlimited imperialism are the expansionist policies of Alexander, Rome, the Arabs in the 17th and 18th centuries, Napolean I, and Hitler, They all wanted to expand their state power towards the establishment of a world empire. Here the lust for power is unlimited and every free state is regarded as an enemy of the goal of world empire. Unlimited Imperialism is considered to be the goal by all such imperial powers who are guided by the irrational desire to dominate and rule all other nations.

Methods of Imperialism/Colonialism

The policy of imperialism involves the attempt to over throw the status quo, that is, the reversal of the power relations between the imperialist nation and its prospective victims. For achieving this, the imperialist nation can adopt three alternative means:

(a) Military means, that is to effect imperialism through military, conquest;

(b) Economic means, that is control through economic exploitation of other peoples, and

(c) Cultural means, that is the displacement of the native culture by one's own culture.

These are the three methods of Imperialism, which Morgenthau has named as military Imperialism, Economic Imperialism and Cultural Imperialism.

Imperialism by the use of Military Power—Military Imperialism. The first and the crudest method, which was employed by most of the conquerors of all times, was military imperialism. In the words of Morgenthau "The most obvious, the most ancient and also the crudest form of imperialism is military conquest. The great conquerors of all times have also been the great imperialists." Military imperialism seeks conquest by means of direct military attack. The great conquerors, like Hitler, Napoleon Louis XIV, Mussolini and many others, used this method of military conquest on the ground that it enabled them to achieve their goal very quickly. But as a matter of fact, this method is the most dangerous because war is a gamble and nothing can be said about its results. As Morgenthau has rightly observed, "Military imperialism is a gamble played for the highest stakes." Very often military imperialism secures negatives and opposed results. A nation seeking to secure imperialism through military conquest very often finds itself imperialised by other states. Nazi Germany waged war to achieve its imperialistic goals but in the process she lost its power and even fell a victim to other imperialistic powers.

Economic Imperialism.

Those superior economic power for pursuing imperialism over weak and poor states is the most rational method of imperialism. In the words of Morgenthau, "Economic imperialism is less obstructive and also generally less effective than the military variety and is, as a rational method of gaining power, a product of modern time." The common characteristics of a policy of economic imperialsm is to exercise economic control over other nations. Through economic means, the imperial power exercises control over the finances and consequently, the policies of other nations. The Central American republics, for instance, are all sovereign states, but their economic life to a very large extent, is dependent upon exports to the United States. This situation makes it possible for the United States to exercise control over these countries.

These nations are unable to pursue for, any length of time, policies of any kind, domestic or foreign, to which the United States would object. Economic imperialism is a concomitant of the age of mercantilist and capitalist expansion. Its outstanding modern example is "dollar imperialism." The 'oil diplomacy' is also a variety of economic imperialism. Through foreign investment, economic aid, loans, multinational corporations, trade and technology monopolies and other such means the rich and powerful nations of the world are today exercising economic imperialism over the poor countries of Asia, Africa and Latin America—popularly called the Third World.

The real aim of the economic aid and loans that the developed nations give to the under-developed nations, is to control their economies and consequently their policies, domestic as well as foreign. The underdeveloped states are politically independent as well as legally full sovereign states but economically these states continue to be dependent upon the rich and developed states, most of which happen to be traditional imperial powers. This situation of political independence coupled with economic dependence has come to be called Neo-colonialism or Neo-imperialism. Economic imperialism is the key instrument of Neo-colonialism.

Cultural Imperialism, while Military imperialism seeks to reverse the power relations through military conquest and economic imperialism seeks to achieve it through economic control, cultural imperialism seeks to change the status quo and reverse the power relations through control over the minds of men. It aims at the control of the minds of men of other nations by impressing upon them the superiority of the culture, ideology and way of life of the imperial power. Cultural imperialism is a subtle means, a psychological method of expanding state power by impressing upon others, through persuasion and propaganda, the superior nature of the culture and ideology of the imperial power. This method of imperialism does not involve the use of either military power or economic pressure but at the same-time is much more effective and enduringly successful in achieving the goal of imperialism. In the words of Morgenthau, "Cultural imperialism is the most subtle and, if it were to succeed by itself alone, the most successful of imperialist policies," American policy of impressing upon other nations the value of freedom, free enterprise and liberal democracy is in fact a subtle method of influencing other nations in favour of American power in international relations.

The Satellite television telecast technology has greatly enhanced the ability of the developed states to attempt a cultural invasion of Asian and African societies. However, in practice as a method of imperialism, cultural imperialism plays a secondary role to other two methods. This method in itself in seldom effective and successful. Its success can be possible only when it is combined with the military and economic methods. Usually cultural imperialism is used to soften up the enemy or states which are the objects of the imperialist policy. It is used as a means for preparing the way for military conquest or for economic penetration into the life of other peoples. Cultural Imperialism is currently designed to create spheres of influence of the developed nations. These are the three popular method of imperialism. Some scholars regard religious imperialism as a distinct and separate method. But we believe that religious imperialism falls under the category of cultural imperialism and hence we have not discussed it separately. While discussing these three methods of imperialism, Morgenthau makes it clear that these should not be confused with the objectives of imperialism. Military conquest, Economic exploitation and Cultural penetration are the means of imperialism. The end is the overthrow of the status quo, that is the reversal of power relations between the imperial power and its prospective victims. These methods should not be confused with the motives of imperialism.

Economic gains are recognised as the important motives of imperialism. Many leftist scholars go to the extent of explaining imperialism solely in terms of economic factors. They hold that imperialism is fundamentally a system designed by the rich nations for economic exploitation of the backward nations. There exist three economic theories of imperialism which seek to offer an economic explanation of the origin and functions of Imperialism.

These are; Marxist-Leninist Theory, The Liberal Theory and The Devil Theory.

The Marxist-Leninist Theory of Imperialism

This theory seeks to explain imperialism as the highest phase in the development of capitalism. Marxian ideas, as interpreted and developed by Lenin, form the core of the theory of imperialism. This theory rests upon the assumption that all political actions spring from economic motives. Consequently, when capitalist societies find that they have exhausted the local domestic markets, they bring political forces into play for achieving the subjugation or subordination of outside areas so that these may be held as controlled markets for selling surplus products and for the investment of capital. In this way imperialism is regarded as the natural expansion of capitalism. The tendency of creating and maintaining ever increasing inequalities, that is inhernt in a capitalist system lead to the development of monopoly capital, that is the control of the finances of the state comes to be monoplised and controlled by a small number of capitalists. The expansion of industries lead to surplus production and the capitalists, in order to increase their profits, become very keen to secure foreign markets for selling their products as well as for getting raw materials. They, therefore, use their strong financial position to force the state to attempt for an expansion of state power beyond its boundaries. These states is compelled by the capitalists to control foreign markets and territories and this leads to imperialism. In this way imperialism is actually a form of capitalistic expansionism.

In the words of Lenin, "Imperialism is the monopoly stage of capitalism." Lenin rejected the view of moderate Marxists like Kautsky and Hilferding that imperialism was the 'preferred' policy of capitalist state. Against this, Lenin believed imperialism is the unavoidable stage of capitalistic expansionism. Lenin gives the example of British imperialism over India. It was the economic wealth of India which the Britishers wanted to exploit. They came as traders but became the rulers. British imperialism was highly exploitive of Indian economy and resources. India was always regarded by the British as a market for getting raw material and for the selling of finished goods. Thus the Marxist-Leninist theory of imperialism is an economic theory of imperialism which explains imperialism as an expansion of capitalism.

Theory of Imperialism

The liberal theory of imperialism accepts that economic factors lead to imperialism. It accepts Lenin's logic that states with capitalist economies very often lead to imperialism and war. However, it does not accept tat imperialism is the natural result of expansion of capitalism. The chief exponent of this theory is John A. Hobson. He holds that imperialism is not the result of capitalism as such but of certain maladjustment within the capitalist system.

In conformity with Marxism, this liberal school diagnoses, the surplus of goods and capital which seek outlet in foreign markets as the root of imperialism. Hobson holds that by adjusting the surplus goods in domestic markets through several economic reforms, like increasing the purchasing power and elimination of over-saving, capitalism can be prevented from developing into imperialism. "It is this belief in a domestic alternative to imperialism," writers Morgenithau, "which in the main, distinguishes the liberal school from Marxism.

The Devil Theory of Imperialism

The Devil theory seeks to explain imperialism as "a result of conspiracy of evil capitalists for the purpose of private gains," they create conditions which compel the following of an imperialist policy by their state. In the words of Morgenthau, "While the extreme Marxists equate capitalism and imperialism, and while the moderate Marxists and the disciples of Hobson see in imperialism the result of maladjustments within the capitalist system, for the adherents of the devil theory of imperialism and war in general amount to nothing but a conspiracy of evil capitalists for the purpose of private gain." The Nye Committee (194-36), which investigated on behalf of the U.S. Senate, the influence of financial and industrial interest on the intervention of the United States in the First World War. Observed that, "certain evil capitalists of groups-munition makers, Wall Street and the like were responsible for seeking war as a means of profit." These war profiteers transform themselves into the "war mongers" the "devils" who plan wars in order to enrich themselves.

Critical Evaluation of the Economic Theories of Imperialism

The economic theories of imperialism have been severely criticised by a number of scholars as unhistorical, partial and inadequate theories of imperialism. These have been criticised mainly on the following grounds:

Unhistorical. These economic theories of imperialism and war fail to stand the text of historical experience and hence are unhistorical. No doubt, some wars of the 19th and 20th centuries, for instance the Boer War of 1899—1902 and the Chaco War between Bolivia and Paraguay (1932-35), were fought for economic objectives, yet the main wars have always been fought for political objectives. During the entire period of mature capitalism, no war, with the exception of the Boer War, was waged by major powers exclusively or even predominantly for economic objectives. The Austro-Prussian War (1865) and the Franco-German

War (1870) had no economic objectives, and The Crimean War (1854-56), the Spanish-American War (1898), the Russo-Japanese War (1904-05), the Turko-Italian War (1911-12) and the Balkans War involved only minor and subordinate economic objectives. The two World Wars were certainly political wars. Wars produced economic advantages for the victors but only incidently.

Imperialism Predated Capitalism. The origin of Imperialism in international relations came much before the coming of capitalism. The main period of colonial expansion, which the economic theories tend to identify with imperialism, came much before the age of mature capitalism and hence cannot be attributed to and explained on the basis of inner contradictions of capitalist system. In comparison with those of the 16th, 17th, and 18th centuries, the colonial acquisitions of the 19th and 20th centuries have been small. The latest phase of capitalism has even been accompanied by a liquidation of imperialism through an international process of decolonialisation.

Imperialism is basically a political doctrine and not an economic device of exploitation. A review of the empires that were traditionally built reveals that Imperialism has all along been a political mechanism of the great conquerors. The policies that, in ancient times, led to the foundation of the Egyptian, Assyrian and Persian empires were imperialistic in the political sense. So were the conquests of Alexander and the policies of Rome in the last century before the Christian era lous XIV, Peter the Great, Napolean I and more recently Hitler were all motivated by political power and prestige in pursuing the policies of imperialism. With them, political considerations were the primary considerations and these were always regarded as superior to economic gains which accrued from imperialism.

Government and not capitalists seeks imperialism. The thesis of the economic theories that capitalism and capitalists always compell the government to follow imperialism, is not supported by facts of history. History gives ample proofs of a reverse relationship between government and capitalists in the context of imperialist policies. Imperialist policies were generally conceived by the governments who summoned the capitalists to support these policies. "Politics has always held primacy over economics." It is a universally accepted fact of international relations. "The rule of the financier...over international politics," writes Schumpeter, "is indeed a newspaper fairy tale, almost ludicrously at variance with facts."

The economic theories of imperialism though appear plausible, are in fact, far away from realities. No one can deny the existence of economic motives of imperialism, but at the same time no one can accept that economic motives are the foundation stones of imperialism. Further more, these theories are superficial in so far as these try to explain a complicated phenomenon like imperialism solely in terms of inherent tendencies or abuses of capitalism.

Critical Evaluation of Imperialism/Colonialism

Since ancient times, imperialism has been a fact of international relations. Before 1945, it was regarded by its supporters as the instrument of international peace and development. A number of arguments were used by the imperial powers to justify their rule and control over other states. Some justified it on the principle of White Man's Burden while others used several arguments to support it. The main arguments that its supporters advanced in support of imperialism can be summarised as under:

Arguments in Favour of Imperialism

A Natural Phenomenon of international relations. Many supporters of imperialism justified is as a natural phenomenon based upon the natural laws of social evolution as "*Struggle for existence," "Survival of the fittest"* and "Will to survive and dominate." On the basis of these laws, it was argued by them that every nation has the inherent right to be more and more powerful to dominate the weaker. Imperialism was regarded as the natural outcome of the relation of these laws in the sphere of international relations. Fascist dictator Mussolini justified his policy of war an imperialism on the basis of these natural laws.

Growing population makes imperialism a natural choice. It has been argued in favour of imperialism that each nation has the duty to satisfy the needs and interests of its population. The ever increasing population of a nation makes it essential for the state to seek new territories for securing essential resources, raw-materials and markets for promoting the well being of its people.

Economic Justification. Imperialism is further justified by its supporters on economic grounds. It is regarded as a valuable means for channelising the surplus goods as well as means for securing raw materials and markets abroad. Imperialism is defended as an ideal means for the uplift of the economically backward people. It involves the concept of economic cooperation between the developed and the backward peoples. Imperialism makes it possible for the people of colonies to enjoy the benefits of industrial and technological advancement through their association with the imperial power.

White Man's Burden. A racialist argument in favour of imperialism has been that it is the responsibility of the 'White Man', being superior and better developed man to help the peoples of other races to develop. It is indeed, argue the supporters of Imperialism, a moral obligation of the White race—'the European's to undertake the task of uplift of the backward and inferior people. It is further observed by many pro-imperialism theorists that, in colonising and imperialising Africa, Asia and other parts of the world, the Europeans have in fact been discharging their moral obligation. It was a duty of the non-white races to accept the 'big-brotherly care' and 'benevolent' rule of the White man.

Imperialism is an Instrument of Political Utility. Another argument in defence of imperialism has been that it is an instrument of political unity of the colonies. Imperialism helps the political consolidation and awakening of the people of colonies. It is asserted that in the company of highly civilised and politically developed people of the imperial nations alone that the people of the colonies can become politically conscious of their rights and duties. Imperialism as such is designed to prepare the people of the colonies for becoming self-confident and self-independent. It is a system of providing vitally important training in self-government to the backward people of the colonies. Praising the role played by British Empire in prompting the values of democracy, liberty and self government, Prof. Barker observes, "While the Empire of Great Britain originally signified overseas expansion for the two-fold purposes of settlement and business, it is revealing a process of sublimation which is leading to the totally new idea of a community of self-government nations based on voluntary adhesion to the English ideas of law and liberty."

Imperialism is an Instrument of international Peace and Cooperation. Finally, the supporters of imperialism justify it as instrument of internationalism, peace and universal brotherhood. Living as parts of an empire makes the people of different colonies develop a sense of unity and partnership. It inculcates among them a spirit of internationalism and brotherhood. Imperialism strengthens peace by making people rise above narrow nationalism an parochialism. In the words of C.D. Berns "Imperialism breaks down the narrowness of village politics and leads to internationalism and brotherhood."

Summing up these arguments in favour of imperialism, it has been observed that, "imperialism brings peace and order out of chaos and confusion, it act as an arbiter among various warring sections of the backward community...it protects the masses against native exploitation...it makes available the unused resources of the country to the world at large...it makes uniform laws over vast territories and in these days of terrific competition for finished goods and markets for raw materials, it is a distinct advantage for countries unable to stand on their own feet to be parts of a large empire which can give them protection and orderly life."

Arguments Against Imperialism

The above arguments in favour of imperialism wrongly and unobjectively project it as an ideal system with strong humanistic motives. These arguments are in reality the product of a coloured vision in favour of imperialism. No amount of logic, except a partial, tailor-made and short-sighted-illogical irrationalism can ever justify imperialism as something natural and good. Imperialism is an evil, rather the evil which has been a source of almost all the ills and evils of our times. It is an in- human, anti-liberal and anti-democratic principle whose real basis, whatever pretensions might be made by its supporters, is the selfishness of powerful nations whose real motive always is to exploit and destroy the native life, resources and culture of the native people for satisfying the selfishness and ego of the people of developed, rich and powerful nations. It is indeed institutionalised immorality which justifies the rule of the superior over the inferior. It artificially and arbitrarily classifies peoples into superior inferior categories. It misuses the name of God in advocating the theory of white man's burden. It debases religion in the name of spreading religion through imperialism.

Imperialism is Inhuman. Imperialism is anti-human because it justifies unnatural and discriminatory inequalities between man and man. It wrongly assumes the superiority of the white race and inferiority of all other races. It gives little respect to the rights and freedom of the dependent people. In the name of such principles like White Man's burden it seeks to violate Human Rights and freedoms of the people of colonies.

Imperialism is Anti-Liberal. It is anti-liberal since it justifies subordination of native people to their imperial exploiters. The thesis of the upliftment and welfare of the people of the colonies as the motive of imperialism is a smoke screen aimed at concealing the selfish, autocratic and authoritarian policies of the imperialists.

Imperialism is Anti-democracy. Imperialism is anti-democracy since its basis is inequality between the imperialist people and the victims of imperialism. It is a sham which pretends to nourish self-government and democracy for the colonies, and which really involves authoritarianism of the worst kind.

Imperialism is a System of Exploitation, Loot and Plunder. Imperialism is a system of organised exploitation of the colonies. It never works for helping the bulk of the population of the colonies. Instead it always helps the imperial masters to gain at the cost of their subjects. Under imperialism, no attempt is made to develop the resources and industrial potential of the colonies. The imperial power is interested only in explaining the colonial resources for its own benefits. Even in respect of the colonial power, only a small elite really gains out of imperialism. In the words of Prof. Schuman "Libya constitutes one of the most perfect examples of colonial possessions, acquired and held at a great cost to the tax payers of the home country for reasons of diplomatic powers and prestige, with only moderate profits accruing to privileged investors and concessionaries, and no economic gain whatever accruing to the nation as a whole." The resources of India were fully exploited by the Britishers for their selfish interest. Imperialism always seeks to vulgarise and exploit the native culture for serving the selfish interests of the imperialists. Ethnic pluralism of India was exploited by the British rulers to keep their empire intact. Divied and rule was practised in the name of protection of minorities. In the name of cultural links and cultural development, an attempt is made to psychologically indoctrinate the people of the colonies in favour of the alien culture.

It seriously hinders the process of nation-building in the colonies. Infact, imperialism creates unnatural inequalities, and by following divided and rule, it attempts to fragmantise the nation into small 'nations' and consequently to perpetuate its control over them. Imperialism is inherently inhuman, anti-liberal, anti-democratic in nature and scope. It is a curse and slur on humanity. Fortunately, the forces of anti-imperialism, anti-colonialism as well and national liberation movements have been successful in liquidating several sins of traditional imperialism and colonialism from international relations of our times. Much, however, still remains to be done. The new force of imperialism-colonialism i.e., neo-colonialism is yet to be eliminated from the international system.

Effects of Imperialism

Almost all parts of the non-industrialized world had come under the direct or indirect control of a few industrialized countries. Most countries of Asia and Africa had lost their political freedom and were ruled by one or other imperialist country. The economies of all these countries as well as of those which were politically independent were controlled by a few imperialist countries to serve their interests. All parts of the world were brought together under a world economic order which was based on the exploitation of the colonies. Since 1946, most Asian and African colonies have become free and independent. You will read about this in detail later. But the effects of imperialism on the life of the people in these countries are still evident.

The most important and lasting consequence of imperialism and colonialism was the economic backwardness of the colonies as well as of those countries which were indirectly controlled by the imperialist countries. Imperialism led to the destruction of local industries in these countries. For example India for. centuries had been an exporter of textiles. During the period of imperialist rule, India's indigenous textile industry was destroyed and she became an importer of British cloth. The natural resources of the colonies came under the control of the imperialist countries and were exploited for their own benefit. The industrialization of these countries was prevented. Where industries were started, these were subordinated to the interests of the industries of the imperialist countries or for making profits for the companies of the imperialist countries. The modern industries in the colonies had little impact on the life of the people there. The patterns of agriculture in the colonies were also changed to meet the requirements of the industries of the imperialist countries. In some countries. The entire agriculture was reduced to the growing of one or two crops. For example, Cuba was reduced to the position of a sugar-producing country and little else. There was also naked plunder of natural resources, and exploitation through high demands of revenues and taxes. Some of the best lands in the colonies were taken over by the European planters. Imperialism further aggravated the economic backwardness of the nonindustrialized countries of the world. The subordination of the economics of these areas to those of the imperialist countries was so complete that even after political independence, most of these countries found it difficult to develop their economics to suit their own interests. The improvement of the people of the colonies and of other non-industrialized countries is a continuing consequence of imperialism.

Imperialism also bred racial arrogance and discrimination The idea of the superiority of the white race whom God had created to govern the world, was popularised in the imperialist countries. In their colonies, the white rulers and settlers discriminated against the local inhabitants who were considered inferior to them. In most European colonies, there was no intermixing with the local population and the Europeans lived in areas exclusive reserved for them. The worst example of racism was South Africa where intermixing of whites and blacks was made a criminal offence. It is interesting to know that when Japan emerged as an imperialist power, the Japanese were excluded from being branded as belonging to an inferior race. Infact South Africa gave the Japanese the status of what they called 'honoracy whites.'

4

De-Colonisation and Resurgance of Afro-Asian Countries

South and South-East Asia includes Nepal, Burma, Sri Lanka, Malaya, Idonesia, Indo-China, Thailand and the Philippines. Even before the rise of the new imperialism, many of these countries were already dominated by the Europeans. Sri Lanka was occupied by the Portuguese, then by the Dutch, and later by the British. England introduced tea and rubber plantations, which came to form seven-eights of Sri Lanaka's exports. The Dutch lost Malaya to the British, including Singapore, lying at the tip of the Malaya peninsula. The conquest of Malaya and Singapore meant control of all the trade of the Far East that passed through the Straits of Malacca.

Indonesia and the surrounding islands were under Dutch control. After 1875, Holland extended her control over a group of islands known as the Moluccas. The area in South-East Asia once called Indo-China consists of Laos, Cambodia and Vietnam. When England was fighting China over the opium trade, France was trying to extend her commerce in Indo-China. In a series of planned steps which included threats of war, France became the master of Indo-China and the separate states were grouped together under a French governor-general. Frequent revolts against french rule followed, but they were suppressed or, as the French said, 'pacified'. Thailand, or Siam, remained an independent state, though sandwiched between the French conquests in Indo-China and of the British in Burma. But France and England exercised much power and authority over its affairs. The United States joined in the race of imperialist expansion in South-East Asia in the late nineteenth century.

In the inter-war period some of the Afro-Asian countries carried on struggle for independence but could not achieve much success. It was only after the Second World War that a number of Asia and African countries gained independence. Through their consistent efforts inside the UN, as well as outside, they succeeded in demolishing the contention of the imperialist powers that racialism was essentially a domestic problem. They fully utilised the forum of the United Nations, the General Assembly in particular, impress on the international community that racialism was an international problem which posed a serious threat to the international peace. It was mainly due to the efforts of the Afro-Asian group in the United Nations that the racialism in South Africa and Rhodesia etc. was debated and the powers practising racialism were censored.

In short, the Afro-Asian countries have been the chief force behind the struggle against imperialism and racialism. The emergence of Afro-Asian countries has given a serious blow to the colonial system. Over 100 states have attained independence since 1945 and majority of them are in Asia and Africa. After their independence these countries extended full support to the nationalist movements elsewhere and succeeded, to a large degree, in getting them free from the colonial yoke, Even at present these states are fully backing the struggle of the people of Namibia against South Africa. In short, the Afro-Asian countries have exerted great influence on the imperialist powers to stage a retreat.

The Afro-Asian countries have also taken a lead in organising struggle against neo-colonialism. It is mainly due to the efforts of Afro-Asian countries that the renunciation of unequal treaties and agreements under which the imperialist powers enjoyed various kinds of privileges, the dismantling of the imperialist bases withdrawal of foreign troops etc. from the neo-colonial countries had been made possible. In fact the Afro-Asian countries are determined to defend their sovereign rights against the former colonial powers in particular and the imperialist world in general.

In the economic sphere also the Afro-Asian countries have made a determined bid to escape exploitation at the hands of the imperialist powers and insisted on establishing economic relations terms of equality. In most of the former colonial countries the foreign property has been nationalised and a determined bid has been made to acquire full control over the natural resources of the country. This has gone a long way in ending the neo-colonial exploitation.

Helped in Strengthening World Peace

India's sincere efforts in maintaining peace in the sub-continent have been reflected several times through its relations with neighbouring countries. In this regard, a special mention of the India-Pakistan Declarations from time to time highlighting peace and understanding between the two countries needs to be mentioned into. Signing of the famous tashkent Declaration of 1966 is one such example. Through this declaration of 1966 is one such example. through this declaration, both the countires affirmed the need for negotiated settlement of disputes.

The Afro-Asian countries have rendered great service to the cause of World peace by adopting the path of non-alignment and keeping off from the power blocs. As most of the Afro-Asian countries were economically backward they wanted to devote their full energy to quicker development of their countries. This naturally demanded that they should keep out of the mad race for armaments and the cold war prevailing in the post World War II period. Further, as they needed financial assistance for their development, it was not desirable on their part of align themselves with one side or the other. On the other hand, they wanted to get the best of assistance from both the groups.

The emergence of a strong non-aligned group went a long way in reducing tension between the two super powers and reducing the gravity of cold war. The best justification for keeping-off from power blocs was provided by Pandit Nehru of Indian thus: "if we camp followers of Russia or America or any other country of Europe, it is, if I may say so, not very creditable to our dignity, our new independence, our new freedom, our new spirit and our new self-reliance." The Afro-Asian countries contributed to world peace not only by keeping out of the two power blocs but also by avoiding war if possible and keeping out of all wars except those undertaken in self-defence; by opposing military pacts because these led to insecurity; and through, collective action and in right direction.

Prominent Role at the UN

United Nations was formed after the end of the Second World War. The horrors of the war terrified the entire humanity. With the noble objective of saving the world form the scourge of another war. United Nations was founded on 24 October, 1945. Originally fiftone naitons became members of the UN. Over the years, the membership of UN has grown. at present, United Nations has more than 191 members. The main cause of increase in membership is the decolonisation of many Asian and African countries. Like other origanisations, UN also has a Charter. It sets down the main objectives of the UN. It sets down the main objectives of the UN. It also lays down the structure of the UN and the functions of its various organs. The headquarter of the United Nations is situated in New York city of U.S.A.

The Afro-Asian countries, due to their numerical strength, have been able to play prominent, rather dominant role in the United Nations. No doubt, in the beginning the Afro-Asian countries were not able to exert much influence on the decisions of the United Nations but with the passage of time and growing cohesion of the anti-colonial and anti-imperialist forces they emerged as a potent force and were able to exert much influence on the political and economic issues. Both the Powers, aware of the voting strength of the Afro-Asian countries have been trying to woo them because they cannot dare to easily brush aside their views. It may, however, be noted that the process of increasing participation of these countries in the international affairs has not been all smooth and the former colonial and imperialist powers have tried to undermine this process through the ruling elites in these countries. But despite these hurdles most of the Afro-Asian countries, because of their experience in the international sphere, developed new confidence and have been able to safeguard their national interests with effectiveness.

The growing role of the Afro-Asian countries at the United Nations and other international forums has met with severe criticism at the hands of imperialist powers. The western countries have often complained that the developing countries are dominating the United Nations by virtue of their sheer physical majority. According to Prof. Vernon Mckay this has complicated the international relations. He says "it creates not only substantive problems but organisation difficulties for all the foreign offices of the world. It brings forth a large group of untrained and inexperienced diplomats dealing with unfamiliar tasks." However, it is not possible to agree with this criticism because the Afro-Asian countries have not complicated the international relations, rather they have strengthened the same. It is different matter that the western powers have not been able to reconcile with the role of diminishing importance. In the past some of the Afro-Asian diplomats might have behaved in an inexperienced manner and even showed some sort of dependence on their senior partners, but now they have acquired sufficient experience in the international sphere and do not any more suffer from lack of confidence and psychology of dependence. They have been able to staff their diplomatic services with people who are capable of safeguarding their national interests.

Peace Efforts through United Nations

As most of the Afro-Asian countries were economically and militarily no match for the big powers they tried to place greater reliance on the United Nations and other international agencies for the solution of various political, economic and social problems. economic and social problems. They have consistently supported UN intervention in the various political issues to ensure that the world peace was not disturbed. In the socio-economic fields too they have insisted on greater role for the United Nations and its agencies. It was mainly due to the instance of the Afro-Asian countries that United Nations set up Special Fund and launched various Technical aid programmes in the various underdeveloped countries with a view to expedite the development of the economies of these countries. But repeatedly expressing their faith and loyalty in the UN Charter and the Universal Declaration of Human Rights these states have succeeded in creating a very favourable climate in favour of the world body. In view of this even the Super Powers have not been able to bypass the UN and have extended full support to it. In short, it will not be wrong to say that the Unite Nations has come to occupy a prominent position chiefly because for the Afro-Asian countries.

New International Economic Order. Ever since their independence the Afro-Asian countries have been insisting on the regulation of economic relations among various nations on terms of equality and have been demanding a say in the determination of the international, commercial monetary and financial policies which effect their interests. But, the imperialist powers were not willing to concede this demand and continued to take important decisions in these matters without consulting them. However, with the increase in the strength of the non-aligned countries, they have come to exert significant influence. In April-May, 1974 and UN General Assembly, at the initiative of the non-aligned countries, adopted a Declaration regarding the establishment of a new International Economic Order and a Programme of Action on the establishment of a New International Economic Order. It was insisted in the declaration that the economic relations amongst the states should be based on the principle of interdependence rather than unequal exchange. It emphasised that the rich and developed countries were obliged to increase and facilitate the flow of resources to the less-developed countries. It was in their own interest to encourage the promotion of growth and development of the poor countries in order to expand their markets. Further progress in this direction was made at the UNCTAD IV Meeting at Nairobi in May 1976 when a programme of global action was adopted to improve market structure in international trade in commodities of interest to the developing countries. Though the goal of new International Economic Order has not been fully achieved as yet, it certainly is an important step in the direction of regulating the international economic relations on the basis of equal distribution of the global resources.

The above discussion clearly establishes that the resurgence of Afro-Asian countries has left a deep impact on international relations. Hoffman has beautifully summed up the significance of the resurgence of Asia-African countries thus; "When the history of the twentieth century is written, it will not be World War I or World, War II, the discovery of nuclear energy, or putting men into orbit, or even an exploration of the moon that is going to be considered as the great event of the century. The outstanding event of this century will be that two-thirds of the world's people awakened to the fact that a better life was possible for them. If we are able thin this century to abolish, as far as is now technically practicable poverty illiteracy and chronic ill-health from the surface of the world the twentieth century, in which we have all lived will go down as the great century of all times."

5

National Power

The concept of power is quite complex and it is not easy to provide a commonly acceptable definition. It shall, therefore, be desirable to discusses some definitions of power reach an acceptable conclusion. Prof. Morgenthau defines political power as "a psychological relation between those who exercise it and those over whom it is exercised. It gives the former control over certain actions of the latter through the influence which the former exerts over the latter's mind". He further states that the struggle for power is unusual in time and space and is an undeniable fact of experience. 'Whatever the ultimate aims of international politics, power is always the immediate aim. According to Schwarzenberger 'the power is the capacity to impose one's will on others by reliance on effective sanctions in case of non-compliances. In the words of Charles P. Schuciche 'power is the ability to exercise such control to make others do what they otherwise would not do by rewarding or promising to reward them, or by depriving or threatening to deprive them of something they value. According to Organiski power is "the ability to influence the behaviour of others in accordance with one's own ends. Unless a nation can do this, it may be large, it may be wealthy, it may even be great, but it is not powerful."

In the broad sense, power can be defined as the ability or capacity to control others and get them to do what one wants them to do and also to see that they do not do what one does not want them to do. Therefore, it is the ability to control the behaviour of other states in accordance with one's own will. The power plays the same role in international politics as money plays in market economy. However, power occupies an important position not only as a means but also as an end. "Power is both the capstone among the objectives which state pursues and the cornerstone among the methods which they employ." (*Vaman Van Dyke*). It is neither good nor evil in itself. "it is socially and morally neutral."

Components of power

What are the factors which contribute to the foundation of power? It is often believed that wealth, resources, manpower and armies are the real foundations of power. But it is not the mere possession of these which makes a nation powerful. It is the possession of certain elements and their skillful use which make a nation powerful. Let us examine those elements which serve as the basis or the foundation of political power.

The importance of the geographical factor, upon which the power of a nation depends, has been recognised since ancient times. The geo-politicians, especially Mackinder and Spykman, have attached great importance to geography Mackinder said. "who rules Eastern Europe commands Heartland, who rules Heartland rules the world islands and who rules world islands rules the world." Spykman likewise says about Rimland "Who controls Rimland rules Eurasia; who controls Eurasia controls the destiny of the world". Most important among geographical factors are the size of country, its topography and location. The size of territory increases the power of a nation. A small state cannot become powerful England was powerful as long as she had colonies. A large state can accommodate a large population and can also have large supply of natural resources on this account. In today's world U.S.A., U.S.S.R., China and India are bound to play effective role in the world, politics. No doubt, the large states like Canada with its frozen wastes, Brazil with its jungles and Australia with its deserts cannot become powerful as a large portion of their territory is not of much use. Vast areas may also add to a nation's power by providing military advantages. The size gives a nation room for manoeuver. Instead of conquerors swallowing the territory it is rather the territory that swallows the conqueror. Napoleon and Hitler failed when they tried to occupy Russia. Similarly, China was saved from total disintegration when Japan attacked it in 1937 on account of its vast size.

The influence of climate on national power is also important. Tropical regions and very cold regions are not suitable for the development of power. The temperate regions are considered the best for the health and energy of the people which lead to the nations, productivity. Similarly uncertain rainfall and periodic draughts also limit the power of a nation. It makes the country increasingly dependent on foreign market for food and obstructs the development of national power and adoption of an independent foreign policy.

Another geographical factor is the location. It determines the country's security. England and Japan being islands have been more secure. Similarly, U.S.A. being separated from Europe and Asia could remain in isolation for a long time. There is a close relation between location and foreign policy. The Middle Fast and continental Europe have been the potential zones of power rivalry because of their geographic and strategic locations.

Topography too plays an important role in the determination of a nation's power. Topographical features determine the natural boundaries between the states and set limit to their natural expansion. The Himalayas have acted as a barrier to Chinese expansion into India. The Pyrenes made a fortress out of Spain, the English channel have guarded the coast of England. Similarly, the British in India could never extend their suzerainty to Nepal because of its typical topography.

However, the geographic factor has lost much of its importance in recent times because of the advancement in science and technology. According to Pedelord and Lincoln. "The astronomical impact of technology in areas such as communications, air mobility. ICBM systems, nuclear weaponary, intelligence gathering space satellites has drastically collapsed the strategic obstacles to the projection of national power."

The natural resources and the raw- materials available in a country also greatly contribute to the national power. While the natural resources are the gifts of nature, the raw-materials are the result of human labour. The natural resources include minerals, flora, fauna, fertility of soil, waterfalls etc. The raw-materials include food, rubber, cotton etc. However, the natural sources do not by themselves create power. They have to be exploited with the help of capital, technical know-how and skilled labour. For example though Brazil had rich iron deposits they did not contribute to her national power till these were exploited with the technical assistance received from USA. Again the power of a nation does not depend on the availability of one or two natural resources, but on the availability of a large number of them. In present times raw-materials like oil, uranium and atomic energy have also greatly affected the national power of the country. Another important natural resource is the foodstuffs. The countries enjoying self-sufficiency in food-grains is likely to be powerful. The strength of USA and USSR is largely due to self-sufficiency in foodstuffs. If a country is dependent on foreign markets for the supply of foodstuffs its independence of action is greatly reduced and its power automatically diminishes. It is well known that the Allies succeeded in bringing down Germany during World War I because she failed to procure foodgrąins from other countries. In India also the government could not pursue any vigorous foreign policy so long the country was dependent for her food supplies on other countries. But once India attained self-sufficiency in food supplies following the Green Revolution, it showed greater independence of action.

The other raw materials which are considered vital for the national power include coal, iron, copper, oil etc. Britain emerged as a great power during the nineteenth century chiefly because of her industrial development, which was rendered possible due to presence of coal and iron ores in abundance. In our own times oil has come to be regarded as an important source of national power. The countries possessing rich oil deposits have come to occupy a position of great influence in the international sphere. The strength of USA and USSR is also greatly due to self-sufficiency in oil resources. Of late the natural gas and atomic energy have also come to be regarded as important sources of national power. It may be again reiterated that the mere presence of natural resources and raw materials is not enough. They contribute to the national power only when they are fruitfully exploited.

Technology implies the application of science and newer methods of production. In recent years technology has come to exercise profound influence on the power base of a state as well as the course of international relations.

Technology atleast in three spheres—industrial, communications and military, has greatly influenced the power of the state. The industrial technology adds to the power of the country by enabling it to increase its production and attaining economic surplus. The transport technology has resulted in improvement in methods of transportation of ideas, people and goods. It has exercised profound influence on the nature of diplomacy and thereby effected the nature of international relations. The diplomats are no longer expected to act on their own and receive full directions from the Foreign office. The military technology has played even more important role in increasing the power of a state it is well known that Britain was able to dominate over vast colonies spread all over the world chiefly due to her military advancement, Similarly, in the post World War II period USA and Soviet Union have been able to acquire supreme positions due to their military and industrial technology, Similarly Japan has emerged as a powerful nation because of developments is industrial technology. In short technological advancement in the various spheres is an important factor in determining the power of a state.

The population is another important contributory factor to the national power. Generally large population is considered a source of strength, but sometimes it can also be a source of weakness for the state. If the state can utilise its human resources effectively and ensure them a decent standard of living and provide constructive outlets for their talents and energies, the large number can be an asset. On the other hand, if a state cannot provide necessities to its large population the same is a source of weakness. Generally large population is a source of strength in the developed countries while in the under-developed countries it is a source of weakness. Emphasising the importance lf large population Mussolini once said "Let us be frank with ourselves. What are 40 million Italians compared with 90 million Germans and 200 million Salvs ? Given that there are sufficient resources available in the country the large population can help in increasing the agricultural as well as industrial production. It is helpful in raising large armies and acquiring effective hold over conquered territories. According to Morgenthau "since size of population is one of the factors upon which national power rests and since the power of one nation is always relative to the power of others, the relative size of the population of countries competing for power and especially the relative rate of their growth desire careful attention." A country with less population than its competitor will view wit alarm a declining rate of growth if the population of its competitor tends to increase more rapidly.

But the strength of the country does not depend on the number of people alone. The quality of the population is even more important. If the population of a country contains too many children and old people they are a liability in so far as they constitute a serious strain on the economic resources of the country. A country with large adult population is assured of a strong labour force and can exploit the available resources more portably. Similarly, if population of a country is engaged in industrial activities the country shall be stronger than the one whose population is primarily engaged in agriculture. Above all the educational background of the people also greatly contributes to the national strength. If the people possess greater technical capacity, ability, they can exercise more effective control over the forces of nature and contribute to the growth of national power.

Quantity alone does not contribution to the national strength. Quality of the population has great bearing on national power. National character and national moral standard both for their elusiveness from the point of view of national progress and for their permanent and often decisive influence upon the weight a nation is able to put in to the scales of international politics." It was due to the national character of the small European nations that for long they could dominate the large Asian and African nations. National morale to contributes towards the national character. National morale is defined as the degree of determination with which a nation supports the foreign politics of its government in peace or in war. In the form of public opinion it provides an intangible factor without whose support no government, democratic or autocratic, is able to pursue its policies with full effectiveness.' In the words of palmer and Perkins 'Morale is a thing of the spirit made up of loyalty, courage, faith, impulse to the preservation of personality and dignity.' In other words, it is the sum total of the individual qualities of men in a nation in the form of their willingness to put the nation's welfare above their own regional welfare. It amounts to willingness to sacrifice. Studies have been made by the sociologists and anthropologists with regard to national character. On the basis of these studies we tend to think of "Germans in terms of thoroughness, discipline and efficiency, of Americans and Canadians in terms of resourcefulness and inventiveness and of Russians in terms of relentless persistence and the English in terms of dogged commonsense." In Russia and Germany there is a strong tradition of obedience to authority of government and fear of foreigners. Hence, Germans and Russians could easily switch over to war and tolerate dictatorial regimes of Hitler and Stalin.

But it would be too much to draw tangible conclusions on the basis of character traits of certain nations National character and national morale are of elusive and instable character. The national character keeps on changing from time to time. The people are willing to subordinate their personal interests to the nation's welfare during war period only, even thought this sacrifice is of equal significance during peace times as well. If a country is wrecked by internal divisions, jealousies and dissorsions it will either not be able to demonstrate any morale or else if there is any moral it will not be effective.

Economic Development

The economic development is another determinant factory of the strength of a country. Mere possession of raw materials does not make a national powerful. Much depends on the capacity of the state to exploit and utilise these resources. For example, U.S.A., U.S.S.R. as well as India have coal and iron deposits, but lack of industrial capacity by India has been responsible for her comparative weak position. The country must have surplus production if it wants to become economically developed. Those nations whose industrial capacity is greater are considered economically developed and therefore powerful. The decline of France as power in comparison to Germany after 1870 was due to her industrial backwardness. Similarly, the Soviet Union became great power after she acquired top level industrial capacity and improved her capacity to wage nuclear war. Prof. Margenthau has emphasized the importance of economic development and the industrial capacity thus: "The technology of modern warfare and communications has made the over-all development of heavy industries an indispensable element of national power. The quality and productive capacity of the industrial plant, the know-how of the working man, the skill of the engineer, the inventive genius of the scientist, the managerial organisation—all these are factors upon which the industrial capacity (economic development) of a nation and hence, its power depend."

Political Structure

Material and human resources and formation of a good foreign policy would prove usefulness if the political structure or the government cannot play its role effectively. The government is required to choose the objectives and methods of its foreign policy in the light of the power available to support them with a maximum success, a sort of balance between resources and policy. The next task of government is to bring the different elements of national power into balance with each other and to 'secure the approval of its people for its foreign policies and domestic ones designed to mobilise the elements of national power in support of them". Whatever type of political structure, a country may have it should be conducive to function effectively in the formulation and execution of foreign policy. The role of the government does not end with the formulation of the foreign policy. It must put that policy in effect.

The policy cannot be effectively executed unless the people of the state cooperate in carrying it out, "whether as soldiers as consumers or merely as tax payers," Consequently, one of the most important jobs of any government is to ensure people's participation. The government can arouse popular support through propaganda, through political parties and through bureaucracy. Once foreign policy is formed and popular support secured, the job of translating it into action begins. Here too the political institutions play a vital role. The foreign policy can be implemented through peaceful means like negotiations and persuasion. This task is performed by the diplomats. The diplomacy plays an important role in this regard and is considered as the key to power. Diplomacy one might say, is the brain of national power, as national morale is its soul". The government also plays an important role in the nation's economy. Without the proper political support a modern industrial system cannot exist.

Further, it is the government which controls and directs the military. The control of government over armed forces is very essential if the state has to play its role effectively as an international power. Ideas and ideological form are the other elements of power. The ideas which a government holds or supports go a long way in determining the extent of popular sympathy and support for it at home and abroad. In the modern world the ideologies of socialism, communism, democracy, liberalism and nationalism have an international appeal, communism for example has won staunch support in one part of the world while it has aroused antagonism and hostility in the other. Ideology is defined by Pedelford and Lincoln "as a body of ideas concerning economic, social and political values and goals which pose action programme for attaining these goals."

Ideology proceeds with certain assumptions about the nature of man and builds up a theory of human history, a moral code of conduct, a sense of mission and a programme for action. It is an action related system of ideas based on a definite view of the world. The ideology gives unity to nation and a sense of common interest to people. It, also helps the government in finding support from the people. Ideologies also serve as good weapon to raise the morale of the people. The ideology is closely linked with national power. Most of the ideologies are concerned with the achievement of power as the immediate goal of foreign policy by explaining and justifying it in ethical, legal and biological terms. They are also used a cover to hide the real nature of the objectives of a foreign policy.

The quality and wisdom of leadership, both political and literary, is another important element of power. In every political system important and crucial decisions are taken by political leaders. They have to determine the proportions in which the allocation of resources should be made between military and civilian programmes. They decide the nature of relations with other states and declare war and conclude peace or treaties of friendship. Their decisions if successful create direct impact on the power of the states. 'A country is bound to be stronger and more powerful if it leaders have the strength of wisdom and intelligence. The word intelligence needs further elaboration. It does not mean the mental ability of political leaders but the activity designed to produce knowledge a knowledge which contributes to the wisdom of governmental decisions covering foreign affairs. The knowledge amounts to objective understanding of the relative strength and weakness vis-à-vis the home state. This knowledge is a power and is most important, particularly in times of war. A government which lacks the knowledge would run the risk of heading towards a catastrophe.

The leadership must be possessed of both the 'wisdom' and the 'knowledge'. This factor has been recognised as element of power since the earliest times. Military preparedness is the most apparent and tangible factor pable of supporting the foreign policy and promoting national interest. The technological innovation, leadership and quality and quantity of armed forces are vital factors in the military preparedness of a state. The technology of warfare have mostly determined the fate of nations for which the inferior side was unable to compensate in other ways. For example, during early phase of first World War, Germany gained superiority over British because of the use of submarines. In the same way today the nations which posses the nuclear weapons have an advantage over their competitors. The quality of military leadership is another factor which has always exercised a decisive influence upon national power. The power of Russia in the 18th century was a reflection of the military genius of Frederick the Great. In the early 19th century Napoleon displayed superior military leadership and emerged victorius is everywhere. Quantity and quality of armed forces is the most important factor in this directions. A nation to be strong must possess a sufficient army composed of highly trained and heavily armed units. A small army may not prove to be effective. Similarly, a very large army, ill-equipped and ill trained, also proves weak. Finally, the national power of a country is greatly determined by the quality of diplomacy persued by the state.

Dimplomacy

According to Morgenthau it is the quality of a nation's diplomacy which gives 'direction and weight' to other elements of national power. A good diplomacy can bring the different elements of national power to bear maximum effect upon those points in the international situation which have a direct bearing on the national interests. Morgenthau highlights the importance of diplomacy thus: Diplomacy...is the brian of national power, as national morale is its soul. If its vision is blurred, its judgement defective, and its determination feeble, all the advantages of geographical location, of self sufficiency in food, raw materials, and industrial production, of military preparedness, of size and quality of population will in the long run avail a nation little. A nation that can boast of all these advantages, but not a of a diplomacy commensurate with them, may achieve temporary successes through the sheer weight of its natural assets. In the long run, it is likely to squander the natural assets by activating them incompletely, and wastefully for the nation's international objectives." However, this view of Morgenthau is not universally shared. A sizeable number of scholars hold that diplomacy has considerably lost in importance in recent years due to the development of rapid means of communications which has reduced the diplomats to the position of dignified clerks. Further the impact of public opinion and the emergence of open diplomacy has also greatly contributed to the reduction in importance of diplomacy. No doubt, in our time diplomacy has suffered a set back due to above noted factors, but it still plays and important role in promoting the national interests.

The result of war cannot provide an adequate criterion

of power because power in the war is not the only kind of power. A nation may be powerful otherwise but may be defeated in the war. One cannot depend upon the results of war as a criterion of the measurement of national power. A victorious nation is not necessarily a powerful nation. Further, even if war were a proper measure of the power of a nation, it cannot be effectively used because quite often the states parties to war are lined up in groups and the weakness of one is counterbalanced by the strength of another. In such a conflict it is difficult to determine the contribution of the individual nation in the victory. Thus the war at the most provides an occasional clue to the relative power of individual states. Another problem posed in the measure of national power of a state is that it is generally based on past experience. We can tell who won it after the controversy but we cannot tell who will win at the time of the commencement of the controversy. As Organski has put it "Looking at a period of years in the past, we can tell which nations were the most powerful, and we can see the shifts in power from one nation to another that have occurred, but we do not know who will be most powerful tomorrow.

It is not safe to assume that a nation's power will remain the same indefinitely." According to Morgenthau the nations commit three types of errors in evaluating their own power and the power of other nations viz. the relativity of power, the permanency of a certain factor and the fallacy of the single factor. When we say that one nation is powerful and the other nation is weak we always imply a comparison. In other words the concept of power is always a relative one. One of the most elementary and frequent error committed by the states is that they neglect the relative character of power and treat it in absolute terms. If a particular nation is powerful today it may become relatively weak tomorrow and some other nations may emerge powerful. This fact must be nor borne in mind while making evaluation of power. Secondly, it is wrong to assume that the factors of national power are permanent and immune from change. On the other hand these factors undergo constant change.

Therefore, one should never view a particular factor as the source of power of a nation in the dynamic, ever-changing character of the power relations between nations. The third typical error made in assessing the power of different nations is the undue weightage attached to a single factor and the neglect of the others. Such single factor can be militarism, geo-politics or nationalism. Geopolitics is a pseudo science erecting the factor of geography into an absolute that is supposed to determine the power. Similar errors are committed when reliance is made upon the other single factors like militarism or even nationalism. Thus we see that the task of evaluation of power is not so simple and miscalculations can prove disastrous. Under-estimation of one's own power and over-estimation of that of other lead to policies of peace and *status quo* while over-estimation of one's own power and under-estimation of that of other leads to policies of war. After examining the various elements of national powers, it shall be desirable to examine the factors which limit the powers of state.

The most important limitations on the national power are the balance of power; international morality; world public opinion; international law and the United Nations. Let us examine these limitations in some details.

Balance of Power

Like checks and balance in domestic politics, in the field of international politics also the power of one nation or a group of nations is used to prevent a particular nation from imposing its will upon others. The common pattern of balance of power are direct opposition and the pattern of competition. In the former, one state offers direct opposition to the other state with a view to preserve *status quo*. In the latter, two nations compete with each other to establish control over the third nation.

The other common methods used to maintain the balance of power are 'divide and rule' compensations and acquisitions, armaments and intervention, alliances and counter alliances and buffer state formation. They are discussed in detail in one of the subsequent chapters. Power is a crude and unreliable method of limiting the aspiration for power on the international scene. Had the struggle for power taken independent course it would have resembled the Hobbesian 'state of war' and 'might would have been the right'. But in the civilized world the struggle for power cannot go unchecked as it is bound to lead to disruption of society and enslavement and extinction of the individual. To preserve the society certain moral precepts have been put forward which the 'statesmen and diplomats ought to take to heart in order to make relations between nations more peaceful and less anarchic, such as keeping of promises, trust in the others word, fair dealing respect for international law, protection of minorities, repudiation of war as an instrument of national policy etc.' That limits the actions of statesmen and diplomats. They do not pursue certain ends and use certain means because of moral limitations. Thus this type of norms of morality impose limitations on the use of power a country possesses to achieve the desired goals.

All the states are expected to observe universally accepted moral code of conduct. This universal code is often described as international morality. Another limitation on the power of a nation, which is more elusive and lacks analytical precision, is the concept of world public opinion. No nation can exercise the power at its disposal to secure its selfish ends in violation of the world public opinion. According to Morgenthau "World public opinion is obviously a public opinion that transcends national boundaries and that unites members of different nations in a consensus with regard to at least certain fundamental international issues." This world public opinion effectively guards the interests of the humanity as a whole whenever any government or nation executes a particular foreign policy which is against the interest of mankind.

Another question which poses itself is that, does such a public opinion exist and does it exert a restraining influence upon the foreign policies of national government? The answer is both negative as well as positive. Modern history testifies that the world public opinion had never acted as a deterrant against any state which insisted on following a particular policy. The Italian attack against Ethiopia in 1936 and Russian suppression of Hungarian revolution is 1956 can be cited as examples, where the public opinion failed to restrain these powers. But this is one side of the picture. The other side of the story is that the answer to the above question can be given in the affirmative. Its proponents quote the example of the formation of League of Nations which was the result of the world public opinion. Similarly, Woodrow Wilson's fourteen points, which were the basis of the peace talks at the end of the first World War and were accepted by nearly the entire humanity regardless of national boundaries as principles for just and enduring peace settlement.

International Law

The sum total of these norms is known as International law. In the field of international relation the exception of national policy for the fulfilment of the national interests requires the use of force. The most common method of use of force is war or threat of war. If each nation uses its power in unlimited terms against her neighbour or opponent, the world society would come to an end. There would be no peace or stability. It would be perpetual state of war and the life would become nasty British and short.' There would be no progress in the field of art or literature, science or technology. To overcome all this a code of conduct in the nature of international law is necessary to limit the national power. International law in the strict sense is not a law, because of certain inherent deficiencies like the absence of a common law making, law enforcing or law adjudicating body. Its implementation is dependent on the will of the states.

The implementation of these laws by consent or use of external force limits the scope of use of national power by any state. Further the international law permits the formation of arrangements called collective security by a group of nations to oppose collectively, in case a particular nation or another group of nations possessed of preponderant power, tries to jeopardise their independence. Here also the object of international law was to impose such limits on the exercise of national power by virtue of which the international society remains intact. Efforts at disarmament through League and U.N. have also limited the national power. This aspect has acquired much importance in our days. An effort has been made through various conventions to control the use of nuclear weapons which have the potentialities to destroy the entire world.

This has inevitably resulted in the curtailment of the national power. The formation of international organisations like the League of Nations and the United Nations has also restrained the power of the states. To understand this point it shall be desirable to have an idea of the objectives of the U.N. which inter alia stipulate "to maintain internal peace and security and to that end to take effective collective measures for the prevention and removal of threats of peace, and for the suppression of acts of aggression or other breaches of peace, and to bring about by peaceful means, and in conformity with the principles of justice and international law, adjustment for settlement of international disputes or situations which might lead to a breach of the peace." The states are expected to act in accordance with the principles stated in the Charter, It is true that the United Nations cannot intervene in the internal matters of any state except when they pose a threat to the peace, but it certainly acts as a check on the unfair and unlimited use of power by the states and hence is a limitation on national power. The record of United Nations since its establishment shows that the organisation has done commendable work not only in the direction of preserving the peace of the world but also limiting the ambitions of the super powers. It is a world forum where the individual grievances can be ventilated in public. It is relevant to mention here that the open forum helps the formation of the public opinion. The operation of the United Nations since 1945 shows that in quite a number of instances it has been successful in restraining the big powers from coming into open conflict. It is largely felt that U.N. is likely to play more effective role in future and thereby limit the powers of nations to the desired extent. According to Organiski power can be exercised by a state in four ways viz. persuasion, reward, punishment and force.

Let us examine these methods in some details. Persuasion is the most common method adopted by the states for the exercise of power. It involves redefinition of the situation by a state by appealing to the sentiments and principles; by highlighting the unknown facts and holding out the temptation of a reward and threat of punishment, Generally this method is adopted by the small powers how lack coercive power. But the big nations can also adopt this method.

Power through persuasion is used through the diplomatic representatives accredited to various international organisations and delegates to various conferences. The offer of rewards by a state is the next method for the exercise of power. The state can offer rewards in various forms such as territory, military aid in the form of weapons, troops, bases or training facilities and personnel etc. the rewards can also be economic in nature and can take form of loans on gifts trading concessions, lower tariffs, access to strategic material, technical assistance etc. Political rewards can also be offered in the shape of grant of political freedom or increased self-government to dependent area, vote in an international organisation, support for another nation's position at an international conference etc. The third method for the exercise of national power is threat of punishment.

It may be noted that this method is quite frequently used in international politics. For an effective use of this method of power. It is desirable that the threat of punishment should be given in advance, because the very threat may have the desired results and prevent actual action. Further, as Organiski has observed "If punishment must be administered, it should be given in such a form that it can be withdrawn once the offending party mends his way to the satisfaction of the punishing power." Punishment can also assume certain other forms viz. unfavourable propaganda, political support for the enemies of the adversary; creation of deliberate inconvenience for the opponent with regard to immigration, trade transport, economic sanctions and even military action. It may be noted that this method is intended to be only a preventive. Finally, the state power can be exercised through use of force. This method is resorted to only when a nation fails to persuade by bribe or threaten its way to desired goal.

6

Foreign Policy of India

The foreign policy helps us to understand the manner in which a nation conducts its relation with other nations and participates in international affairs on the basis of safeguarding its national interest. National interest pertains to national security, territorial integrity, development issues, economic development, etc. It is also concerned with such global issues as peace, human rights, disarmament, terrorism, etc. In other words, a foreign policy is the sum total of the principles, interests and the objectives of a nation in conducting its relations with the rest of the world. Any change in the foreign policy comes with a change in national interests and global concerns brought about by internal or external factors. The foreign policy of a nation is influenced by many factors such as its geographical position, historical experiences, political traditions, economic compulsions, cultural foundation, constitutional system, national character and the charisma of its leaders' personality. The roots of India's foreign policy can be traced back to its freedom movement with the impact of Gandhian principles and Jawaharlal Nehru's personality.

The foreign policy of India also grew in response to the changes and events of the world. During the British rule, India's foreign policy was given a shape by the Indian

National Congress and the leaders of our country. The desire of the Indian people to live in peace and friendship with their neighbours and other countries was expressed at the Haripura Session of the Indian National Congress in 1938. The ideals of peace, non-violence and co-operation were propounded by Mahatma Gandhi. After Independence, Pandit Jawaharlal Nehru was not only the Prime Minister for the first 17 years, but was also the Foreign Minister of India. As such he was the chief architect of free India's foreign policy

Allegiances generally means devotion or loyalty especially to a person or group entitled to obedience or service and respect. The policy of allegiance came into being after the second world war with the emergence of two super power rivalry on the international affairs. In order to strengthen themselves, USA and Soviet Union started looking for allies who would come under their leadership. As such various countries in the third world began to come allegiance to one or the other super power to fulfil their national objective. They felt that such an allegiance would bring in the much needed foreign aid as well as fulfil the objective of national security—by gaining arms and other equipment to deal with any external aggression. They also started to look to the superpower for guidance, support and assistance. However such a policy of allegiance give the superpower amples scope to interfere in the internal affairs of the satellite states and does lead to the loss of sovereignty. Any sign of refusal to follow the wishes of the leader means the stoppage of all aid and support. The policy of allegiance hence can be said to possess the following characteristics.

Firstly, allegiance to a great power necessarily means that in case of any aggression, the former automatically, moves in to give all financial and arms aid to ward off the aggressor, or if not directly, definitely, indirectly.

Secondly, this system envisages the dominance of the

superpower over its allies. The weaker states have to follow all the wishes of the leader, even if it harms its own sovereign interests.

Thirdly, allegiances are normally followed by the weaker nations in order to gain material gains in terms of aid and arms and also for security aspects. Allegiances became widespread after the cold war and all parties to local wars has been indirectly supported by the two rival superpowers, against one other, e.g. Korea, Viet Nam, Iran—Iraq.

Isolationism

The policy of isolation is a strategy which aims at avoiding such transaction as may be detrimental to the security, liberty and welfare of the nation. The states generally adopt this policy in view of the topographical characteristics, freedom of action, freedom from international complications and tensions, and economic necessity. The policy of isolation is not the policy of isolating oneself from the rest of the world. It only means to avoid the pitfalls of international relations which may jeopardise the national interest. Prior to First World War Japan practised the policy of isolation to stop barbarian infiltration. Japan desired to stop the Western powers from meddling with the Japanese affairs. The Monroe Doctrine of 1823 was again designed to keep off European states from Latin American states and to warn the American policy makers not to pursue a suicidal policy of meddling in European affairs. The topographical characteristics of Nepal and proximity of two big powers to its borders have forced Nepal to opt for the policy of isolation.

During any era of American history, isolationism comprised a coherent body of foreign policy principles. From the time of Washington's Farewell Address, there has always been a tendency to define it by reference to concrete policy issues that the United States confronted in its foreign and domestic affairs. There were several levels of isolationist thought emphasised America's geographic separation from other continents, particularly Europe. It laid stress mainly on America's spiritual and philosophical separation from Europe, pointing out the contrast between the progressive American way of life and the stagnant social and economic system of Europe. It adverted to the fundamental, political and ecological distinctions between the democracy of the New World and the authoritarian political systems and ideologies of the Old World. After 1900, it denoted America's relative military security and invincibility in the Western Hemsphere.

Connotations of Isolationism

The core idea of isolationism was diplomatic and military non-involvement. In the analysis of the several specific facts of isolationism, we must recognise the fact that the concept did not comprise a universally accepted or internally consistent set of foreign policy of guidelines. However, the most widely accepted definition of isolationism throughout the course of American history was the idea of diplomatic and military non-entanglement. This core meaning was illustrated by President Jefferson's admonition in 1801 against "entangling alliances". The phrase "no entangling alliances" in time became the watchword of isolationism. Adherence to the principle of "no entangling alliances" was designed to safeguard the new American republic against the specific danger of involvement in the French Revolutionary and Napoleonic Wars. The risk existed that Americans would find themselves entangled in European struggles in which their interests were secondary to the more powerful European nations and in which their capacity to affect the outcome was minimal. In time the injunction against entangling alliances came to be universalised and raised into a law. The tendency was to interpret and apply it far more rigidly and indiscriminately than its early advocates had intended.

However, we should bear in mind that the principle was enunciated in response to a particular set of circumstances which appeared to threaten the security and well-being of the young in American democracy. As the threat arose from the machinations of European powers, isolationism aimed at the prevention of American involvement in European conflicts.

Isolationism meant the preservation of national sovereignty and independence in decision-making. A closely related connotation of isolationism from the infancy of the republic to the period of the Second World War was the preservation of national sovereignty and independence in decision-making. The United States should avoid entangling alliances with more powerful states, because as a weak and vulnerable country, its independence might be endangered by close diplomatic and military association with more powerful nations. The Munroe Doctrine was directed against the threatened interaction of Holy Alliance in Latin America. The paramount concern of President Munroe was the security and independence of the United States. Invited to join with Great Britain in asserting the concepts contained in his doctrine, Munroe refused. Secretary of State John Quincy Adams maintained that a joint declaration with the vastly more powerful Britain would have reduced the United States to a secondary position.

The dominant connotation of isolationism was unilateralism: During the twenty years following the First World War, the dominant connotation of isolationism was unilateralism. Paul Seabury, in his Power, Freedom and Diplomacy defines this facet of isolationism as the "preference for autonomous action in world politics and a disinclination to be bound by alliances or by any supranational agreements committing the nation in advance to which might involve the use of force or war." In 1924 Secretary of State Charles Evans Hughes declared that although the United States was willing to participate in certain forms of international collaboration, like arms reduction' it "would not tolerate the submission of such questions which pertain to our own policy to the determination of any group of Powers". As war clouds gathered in Europe after the Italian invasion of Ethiopia in 1935, the Roosevelt Administration tried to take limited steps to prevent further aggression. But it took care to avoid being led by the League of Nations. Irrespective of what America's particular response to Axis expansionism, she was required to act unilaterally.

The isolationist heritage precluded her from using her military, economic and moral influence abroad in concert with other nations. Isolationism insists upon America's non-participation in foreign wars. Another component of the isolationist credo was its insistence upon America's non-participation in foreign wars. President Munroe in laying down his doctrine declared.' "In the wars of the European powers in matters relating to themselves, we have never taken any part, nor does it comport with our policy to do so. It is only when our rights are invaded or seriously menaced that we resent injuries or make preparation for our defence," America's desire to escape involvement in foreign wars was a determination which had evolved out of the American experience during the colonial period and the early years under the Constitution. Down to the Second World War, the connection between the staunch adherence to a policy of isolationism and non-participation in war was closed.

Considerations of domestic politics played an important part. If the Americans could successfully avoid becoming embroiled in foreign conflict they could escape such evils as infringement upon their country's independent decision-making by more powerful states, a tendency towards militarism at home, the possible loss of liberties incorporated in eh Bill of Rights and higher taxes.

Comparison between isolationism and non-alignment. Three points of similarity. (1) Both the U.S. and the Afro-Asian nations were militarily weak. (2) Both did not want to be drawn into conflicts, extraneous to their interests. (3) Both were preoccupied with domestic concerns. Isolatonism remained America's avowed foreign policy position throughout the greater part of its experience as an independent nation. This fact provides strong proof that isolationism served American interests in external affairs. The policy of non-alignment followed by the new states of Asia and Africa and America's traditional policy of isolationism reveal many similarities. The new nations of Asia and Africa found themselves in the same position as America in the eighteenth and nineteenth centuries. Three points of similarity between the two are noteworthy. (1) Like the U.S.A. in the early years, the new nations of Asia and Africa were weak and militarily weak for a prolonged period of time (2) They did not want to be drawn into conflicts between the two superpowers which they regarded as extraveneous to their interests and detrimental to their security. They were especially concerned about the participation in the two alliance systems of the U.S.A. and the U.S.S.R. Such a participation in their view would carry the risk of losing their independent decision-making capacity. Their experience in their colonial days was similar to that of United States. For they had been pawns in the conflicts between Great Powers for many years before their independence. (3) Like the United States, the new Afro-Asian states after achieving their independence were greatly preoccupied with their internal concerns, such as strengthening the bonds of national unity, economic development and modernisation of their traditional societies. The elites of the new nations were convinced that the future of their countries depend upon the successful solution of internal problems. Both for the Afro-Asian nations in the contemporary period and for the United States during much of its history, a position of non-alignment, or of isolationism was natural, if not an inevitable stance in foreign policy. In other words, non-alignment or isolationism met their internal and external requirements extremely well. No other diplomatic position could have served their purpose.

USA's Policy

For a long time, before World War I, U.S.A. had been following a policy of isolation. Even when the First World War broke out the majority of Americans were in favour of keeping aloof from the war which did not directly concern them. President Wilson of America even made a declaration regarding America's neutrality. In his message to the American Senate he said "The United States must be neutral in fact as well in name...we must be impartial in thought as well as in action, must put a curb upon our sentiments." It may be noted that this policy of neutrality was in keeping with the traditional policy followed by U.S.A. for many centuries. This policy was first advocated by President Washington in his famous Farewell address when he warned his country to avoid 'entangling alliances' with the governments of Europe. Psychologically, also the American people were inclined to follow the policy of neutralism and non-alignment because they felt that a common man gained nothing from the war and had to pay heavy price. Further America wanted to concentrate all her attention on the economic development.

The wars and the large armies needed for the conduct of the war caused a heavy strain on the economic resources as well as the manpower resources of the country and thereby hampered the economic development. Consequently, the American leaders paid more attention to the economic development and did not bother about political power or glory in the international sphere. During the initial years of the First World War U.S.A. preferred to follow a policy of neutrality even though her sympathy fully lay with the Allies. It adopted an attitude of 'watchful waiting'. But as the war progressed and Germany announced the policy of destroying of enemy ships found in the water about the British Isles without regard to the safety of those abroad the ship, U.S.A. strongly protested. Despite these protests in May 1915 the German submarines destroyed an unarmed English Liner *Lusitania* which resulted in the death of 1200 persons, including 128 American citizens. This incident greatly shocked the American public opinion and a pressure was exerted on President Wilson to declare war against Germany. However, Wilson did not favour going to war with Germany. He was satisfied with the guarantees offend by Germany that in future "Linears will not be sunk by our submarines without warning and without safety of the lives of non-combatants." Germany lived upto this guarantee during the next nine months and no untoward incident took place.

On the other hand Wilson made efforts to end the war through negotiations. The things took a serious turn following a declaration by the German Government in January 1917 that "it would sink at sight all ships, neutral as well as belligerent, in certain waters about the British Isles and in the Mediterranean Sea." No only this by Ist April 1917 eight American vessels were actually destroyed by the Germans which resulted in the loss of 48 lives. Consequently, on 2nd April 1917 Wilson declared in Congress "Neutrality is no longer feasible or desirable when the peace of the world is involved and the freedom of its people threatened...The world must be made safe for democracy. Its peace must be planted upon the test foundations of political liberty. We have no selfish ends to serve. We desire no conquest, no domination. We seek no indemnities for ourselves, no material compensation for the sacrifices we shall freely make. We are about one of the champions of the rights of mankind.

It is a fearful thing to lead this great peaceful people into war, into the most terrible and disastrous of all wars, civilisation itself seeming to be in the balance. But the right is more precious than peace and we shall fight for the things which we have always carried nearest to our hearts, for democracy, for the rights of those who submit to authority to have a voice in their own governments for the rights and liberties of small nations, for a universal domain of right by such a concert of free peoples as shall bring peace and safety to all nations and make the world itself at last free.

This declaration was approved by the Senate on 4 April, 1917 and by the House of Representatives on 6 April 1917. The entry of United States in the war on the side of the Allies titled the balance in their favour. At the time of her entry America had expected that the Allies would need only financial and naval assistance, but soon she realised that the Allies needed money, ships, supplies as well as men to defeat the Central Powers. U.S.A. met all these needs of the Allies and greatly contributed to the defeat of the opponents. U.S.A. sent, roughly, two million soldiers to Europe while her navy cooperated with Britain in meeting the German submarine attacks. The American troops played a dominant role in the decisive second battle of *Marne*. The participation of the American soldiers had a distinct advantage for the Allies. It placed at their disposal the services of soldiers who were not war weary and were still fresh. American also provided huge sums of money to the Allied powers.

The total Allied debt at the end of the war stood over $ 10,000,000,000. It would not be wrong to assert that the support extended by U.S.A. in men, money, food stuffs, minerals and other material resources etc. Greatly contributed to the ultimate victory of the Allies. After Ist World War, United States was convinced that it was a folly on her part to have joined World War I and she was determined to keep out of the new entanglements at all costs. Therefore, it once again returned to her traditional policy of neutrality in the European affairs. After the rise of Hitler this policy of U.S.A. became all the more pronounced. In 1934-35 a Committee of Senate in its report revealed that America was led into First World War by the armaments manufacturers and bankers for purely selfish reasons. In the light of these findings the Congress decided that necessary precautions should be taken to ward against such an eventuality in future. Accordingly, it enacted necessary laws to prevent America's involvement in the hostilities even if it meant that the aggression had to go unchecked. Between 1935 and 1939 Congress passed three Neutrality Acts.

The First Neutrality Act passed in August 1935 forbade the export of arms, ammunition and implements of war from USA to the beligerant states. The Neutrality Act passed in 1937 laid down the principle that all the business will be transacted by USA on 'cash and carry basis,' This meant that the raw materials were to be released only on the receipt of cash price and were to be carried by the belligerent ships. The Neutrality act of November 1939 was the last act passed with a view to preserve America's neutrality. It provided that whenever the American President or Congress found that there existed a state of war between the foreign states and it was necessary to promote the security of the United States or to protect the life of American citizens, the names of the states involved would be announced. After such an announcement it was to be unlawful for any American vessel to carry any passengers or any article or material to any such state.

The American citizens were not to provide any loans to the nations at war. The American citizens were also instructed not to travel on ships of belligenrent states. These laws of neutrality were fully observed during the war between Italy and Abyssinia (1935-36) as well as Spanish Civil War based on the principle that whatever happened outside the borders of the United States, was not the concern of United States. It was not to discriminate between the aggressor and the victim and was to take care of its own interests. It may be noted that these laws were fully observed during the war between Italy and Abyssinia (1935-36) as well as the Spanish Civil War. But in view of the growing tension and international disputes, when the danger of another war loomed large, it became doubtful if United States could really keep out of the war. Accordingly as the war progressed and the western democracies suffered a setback. United States made modifications in her Neutrality laws and permitted the belligerents to buy arms and ammunitions in United States on 'cash and carry' basis. As England and France alone controlled the sea routes, this concession could be availed by them alone. Therefore it can be said that this was an indirect way of helping these two countries against Hitler. U.S.A. formally abandoned this neutrality in 1941 following attack of Pearl Harbour by Japan. At the time of joining the Second world War President Roosevelt told his countrymen. "It will not only be long war, it will be a hard war. The U.S.A. can accept no result save victory, final and complete. We are going to the war, and we are going to win the peace that follows. And in the dark hours of this day and through dark days that may be yet to come, we will know that vast majority of the members of the human race are on our side. Many of them are fighting with us.

All of them praying for us, for, in representing our cause, we represent theirs as well our hope and their hope for liberty under God."

Critical Evaluation of Isolationist Policy

- The success of isolationism enabled USA reduce military expenditure to minimum.

- Isolationism was vital to the solving of domestic issues. Americans were more concerned about domestic political stability, internal unity and social cohesiveness than about foreign relations with European powers.
- America was a nation of ethnic minorities that migrated form Europe into America from 1880s to 1920s. Isolationism was the only policy likely to get support from ethnic minorities in the United States.

The Disadvantages of Isolationism

This historic American policy of isolationism also had certain major disadvantages. These became pronounced after the U.S.A. emerged as a great power in the twentieth century. There were distored or uniformed interpretations of Washington's Farewell Address and Munroe Doctrine which were the sources of isolationist foreign policy. For many local supporters did not take an effort to understand the historical context in which such statements were issued.

- Isolationism which was a response to a particular combination of forces thought to be inimical to the national security became in course of time of universalised formula.
- Belief in isolationism made Americans neglect their national security.

It is difficult for the contemporary student of American foreign policy to evaluate the traditional isolationist point of view sympathetically. While at present very few Americans subscribe to an avowedly isolationist position, the nation's more or less consistent adherence to an isolationist stance for over a century and a half probably affected the American approach to foreign relations after World WAR II, as well as before it. The isolationist doctrine may not be in vogue but many of the assumptions, preconceptions, popular images, attitudes and sentiments associated with the isolationist mentality for more then one hundred and fifty years remain deeply embedded in the American ethos and continue to affect the thinking of the American people and their leaders about events outside their borders. Since 1945 there has been a remarkable continuity between the reacton displaced by Americans towards developments overseas and the assessment of Americans in the mid-nineteenth century or during the 1930s.

Since 1945 America has intervened in political and ideological controversies far from its shore. The most significant military intervention in South East Asia, the Vietnam War, and its failure have persuaded many Americans that such adventures were indefensible. For America's involvement in such crisis will in the end make no difference to their outcome. The critics of American involvement in the prolonged Vietnam conflict contended that it did not lie within the power of the United States to determine the result of political contests in Vietnam. The same conviction underlay the thinking of early isolationists with regard to American involvement in European political rivalries. While isolationism is no longer a doctrine commanding the overall support of the American people, an understanding of the traditional isolationist mentality yields many insights that can be applied to the American approach to foreign relations in the contemporary period.

Nationalist Universalism

Nationalistic Universalism is the international attempt of a nation to impose its own way of life upon others. It began with President Wilson's attempt to make the world safe for democracy. After the Russian Revolution of 1917, the alternative crusade for peace and justice began. After the rise of the two super powers nationalistic universalism has become an attempt to impose on the international scene either the democratic, or the communist, way of life.

This policy envisages that a nation-state wants to play an active role in international affairs. It is a direct contrast to the policy of isolation where the state takes no interest nor involves itself in the world affairs. However, to play a dominant role in international relations, the state needs to possess certain conditions. According to Schewarsenberger, firstly, the state should possess military might, only then will it be able to establish its superiority over other states. Secondly, it must follow an ideology which provides it with the necessary impetus and self confidence to play a dominating role in world affairs. Finally, it must have in its means the technological superiority and advancement which is needed not only to establish its superiority over others but also retain it.

The difference between the nationalism of the nineteenth century and the nationalism of the late twentieth century: Nationalism today is nationalistic universalism. Two types of national conflicts in the nineteenth century.

Today, nationalism has become a universal phenomenon and it has spread to Asia and Africa when it was unknown in the nineteenth century, since the people in Africa and Asia were under the colonial rule of the West European powers and were feeling the impact of modernization. In the nineteenth century nationalism was essentially a European phenomenon. Germany and Italy were late comers as nation states to the comity of European nations. National conflicts in the nineteenth century Europe were of two kinds. First, there were conflicts between a nationality and its alien master. There were conflicts between the Balkan nations and Turkey, between the Slav nations of the Danube basin and the Hapsburg Austro-Hungarian monarchy and between the Poles and the Finns, on the one hand, and Romanv Czarist empire, on the other. Secondly, there were conflicts between the Germans and the French and between the Italians and the Austrians and the delimitation of their respective boundaries. Thus international conflicts in the nineteenth century grew out of these two types of national conflicts. Statesmen hoped that the Paris Peace Settlement made after the First World War would end all such national conflicts that plagued the nineteenth century Europe, since the aspirations of all subject nationalities for nation states of their own were fulfilled. Woodrow Wilson's principle of national self-determination was expected to create a society of satisfied nations and to find the means for their own preservation.

The nationalism of today is nationalistic universalism which claims the right to impose its own standards upon all other nations.

This nationalism which inspired the oppressed nationalities of the nineteenth century to fight for their independence is no longer the nationalism that drives the two super-powers today in their struggle for global supremacy. The nationalism of today, as Morgenthau points out, is really "nationalistic universalism." From the point of view of each of the two super-powers, it is either Pax Americana or Pax Sovietica. The one common point between the new nationalism and the old one is the ultimate point of reference for political loyalties and action." Otherwise, the two are different the area of super-powers dominating the politics of the world and reducing all other nations either to the level of satellites or to the level of second-rate powers, was unknown in the nineteenth century. There were at least six great powers who claimed equal status. Secondly, in the nineteenth century the nation was both the starting and the end-point of all political action. Beyond one nation there were other nations limiting political action. But the nationalistic universalism of the twentieth century begins with the nation as the starting-point of a universal mission whose goal is the domination of the world.

Morgenthau's distinction between the two types of nationalism: Morgenthau brings out clearly the distinction between the nationalism of the nineteenth century and the nationalistic universalism of the late twentieth century in his Politics Among Nations. He observes, "For the nationalism of the nineteenth century the nation is the ultimate goal of politics, the end point of the political development beyond which there are other nationalisms with similar and equally justifiable goals. For the nationalistic universalism of the late twentieth century the nation is but the starting point of a universal mission whose ultimate goal reaches to the confines of the political world. While nationalism wants one nation in one state and nothing else, the nationalistic universalism of our age claims for one nation and one state the right to impose its own valuations and standards of action upon all the other nations."

The characteristics of nationalistic universalism: One particular feature of nationalistic universalism is that it is not connected with any particular nation as the imperialism of the nineteenth century was connected with a particular nation, such as the British or the French nation. For it stems from its universalistic aspirations. For example, the universalistic nationalism of the Soviet Union is not linked with the Great Russian chauvincism but rests on communism. The universalistic nationalism of the Soviet Union has been the instrument for spreading communism throughout the world. Soviet Russian has been using communism since 1945 to transform the world n her own image. Similarly, the United States has been using the democratic ideology as a vehicle for transforming the world in her own image. If China becomes as powerful as Russia or the United States, she may practice universalistic nationalism in Asia with a view to making Asia communist, Thus universalistic nationalism differs from the nationalism of the nineteenth century which was tied to the aspirations of a particular nation and did not take upon itself the role of an evangelist.

Pointing out the differences between the two, Morgenthau observes, "The nationalistic universalism of our age is different in these respects. It is a secular religion, universal in its interpretation of the nature and destiny of man and in its Messianic promise of salvation for all mankind. A particular nation will bear its torch at any particular time, but in principle any nation can. Thus the claims to universalism in the name of the new crusading nationalism may shift from nation to nation according to the conditions of spirit and power."

The dictionary meaning of Pax is a period of international history characterised by an absence of major wars and a general stability of international affairs, usually resulting from the pre-dominance of a specified political authority (during Pax Britannica of the 19th century a vast empire of trade was built up).

The three significant manifestations of nationalistic universalism are Pax Britannica (The Peace of Britain) Pax Americana (The Peace of American or the United States) and Pax Sovietica (The Peace of the formerly Soviety Russia). Of these three phenomena of international politics, Pax Britannica has become a matter of historical interest, since Great Britain after the Second World War lost her empire and, with it, her great power status. She has become a purely European power, having surrendered her leadership in diplomacy and world politics to the United States which with the acquisition of a vast nuclear arsenal has grown in international stature as a super power.

Pax Americana and Pax Sovietica, represented by the United States and the then Soviet Union respectively, are contemporary phenomena of international politics. Each championed the cause of an ideology and wanted to remake the world according to certain set principles in which they believed deeply. Each carved out a sphere of influence in Europe and contended for power and influence in the

Third World. The rivalry between the U.S. and the former Soviet Union, the two super powers dominating the world was in fact, arivalry between the two ways of life, one the liberal democratic way represented by Pax Americana, and the other the Marxist or Communist way represented by Pax Sovietica.

Pax Britannica: The general character of the British foreign policy in the 19th was determined by the immutable conditions of her geographical situation on the ocean flank of Europe as an island state with vast overseas colonies and dependencies. Britain, during that time sought to maintain a balance of power on the continent of Europe, a policy dictated alike by self interest and by the desire to be on friendly relations with other nations. For this purpose England intervened in continental affairs again and again, usually in support of the state or coalition of states which was prepared to resist the dominant power of the day. England regarded herself as the holder of the balance of power.

Great Britain was long the greatest of imperial powers. It could never have played such a dominant role in international affairs in the absence of large number of colonies and dependencies away from home.

Together with these factors was that Britain was the first country to achieve Industrial Revolution. Her leadership in Industrial Revolution, in international finance and in world trade brought her all the pomp and glory in world affairs.

This glorious period in British power was known as Pax Britannica. However British power slowly began to decline. The rise of USA and Japan signified new and powerful non-European rivals appeared to challenge Britain's political, commercial and Naval supremacy. The unification of Germany under Bismark and her ambitious ventures under William II introduced another economic and naval competitor for Britain.

The decline of the power was gradual and its full implications came about only after the second world war.

After the Ist World War, Britain lost its dominance in world affairs with rising nationalism in North East, Middle East and in India. Independence movements began in the British colonies and freedom struggle become strident. Until World War I. Britain had sought to preserve the Ottoman empire however it broke up and Britain no longer could fulfil her dominant role in Middle East. After the second world war, a power vacuum was created in the area which USA and Soviet union filled up.

With more and more colonies gaining freedom and losses of British power in international trade and commerce and the inability to act as the balancer of power, the period of Pax Britannica came to an end.

Two manifestations of Pax Britannica: (1) As an imperial phenomenon bringing law and order/and the blessings of the rule of law to the conquered peoples of Asia and Africa; (2) As an international phenomenon of maintaining the balance of power.

After finally destroying the French colonial rivalry in the French Revolutionary and Nepolenic wars Britain emerged as an unchallenged imperial power in South and South East Asia. She defeated local kings and chieftains and gradually extended her rule over the Indian sub-continent. The British imperialist historians justified the British conquest of India and imperial rule in terms of peace and order and security of person and property. The benefits which the conquered people enjoyed under the British rule were described as Pax Britannica. A constrast between the conditions prevailing before the British conquest and those after it was drawn to justify Pax Britannica. Before coming under the British rule, the country was in a state of disorder and there was no security of life and property. Thugs and other dacoits disturbed the peace of the land. The Cornwallis Code laid the foundations of orderly government procedure and of the rule of law. However, Pax Britannica was an argument for the permanent British rule over Indians.

Both in Asia and Africa Pax Britannica meant the cultural penetration of the western values into the traditional societies of the Asian and African peoples. The British introduced a secular, Western system of education with English as the medium of instruction. A new class of English educated Indian believing in the Western political ideas of liberty and equality arose and it demanded the introduction of representative and responsible government in India.

Early Indian Marxists, like Rajni Palme Dutt, attached the concept of Pax Britannica on the ground that it not only justified the British imperial rule but was harmful to the interests of Indians. For India was kept underdeveloped as a country producing raw materials for British industries. There was no promotion of Indian industries. Pax Britannica meant permanent colonial dependence.

(2) Pax Britannica as an international phenomenon of maintaining the balance of power. Factors contributing to the British supremacy.

The halcyon days of British imperialism were in the nineteenth century when the naval supremacy of Great Britain was unchallenged. She defeated Napoleon Bonaparte's attempt to establish the French supremacy on the continent. The Congress of Vienna (1815) assured Pax Britannica in Asia and paved the way for colonial penetration into Africa. The period between the Congress of Vienna (1815) and the

First World War (1914-18) is the glorious period of what the British historians call the Pax Britannica. During the period Britain played the dominant role in European politics and preserved the balance of power in Europe. A favourable combination of historical circumstances enabled Britain to obtain a leading position in international politics. America was following an isolationist policy and was recovering from the consequences of the Civil War. The Melji restoration in Japan was laying the foundations of modern Japan. Italy and Germany attained their unity in 1871 and Germany had not yet challenged British naval supremacy. The rise of Germany and the defeat of Nepoleon III and the collapse of the Second Empire compelled France to abandon her traditional enemity of Britain and look to her former enemy for help against the German threat. Palmer and Perkins in their book, International Relations, summarise the factors that made Pax Britanica possible in the nineteenth century. They were "England's leadership in the Industrial Revolution, in international finance, and in world trade; her navy, which gave her control of the seas and free access to her widespread possessions and to the markets of the world; and the post-Nepoleonic situation in Europe which gave Britain no formidable challenger to her unique position until the rise of Germany".

The decline of Pax Britannica. Factors contributing to its decline: During the period of her supremacy Britain faced two challenges and successfully resisted them. Her control over the Suez Canal and the Eastern Mediterranean Sea was vital for the maintenance of the sea lanes to the British empire in Asia. So she supported Turkey against the aggressive designs of Czarist Russia. She fought against Russia in the Crimean War (1954-56) in support of Turkey when Russia threatened Constantinople. The second challenge was from imperial Germany. The Franco-Prussian War of 1870-71 ended in the collapse of the Second Empire of Nepoleon III and the rise of the Third Republic of France. The southern

Catholoic German states united with the northern Protestant ones and Bismarck achieved the unity of Germany under the leadership of Hohenzollern Prussia in 1871. The rise of imperial Germany meant the displacement of France as a leading European power. Germany started competing with Britain for markets and colonies. She began building warships and threatened the naval supremacy of Britain. Germany now threatened the balance of power in Europe.

At the beginning of the twentieth century, America and Japan became developed industrial countries and competed with Britain in world markets. Americas dollar diplomacy in the western hemisphere undermined Britain's economic position in Latin America. Though Britain in alliance with France and Czarist Russia was able to defeat the continental powers of Germany and Austria-Hungary in the First World War (1914-18), she could no longer play her old dominant role in world politics after the Peace of Versailles (1919). In the Far East, Japan rose to be a great power and captured Manchuria in violation of all international norms. The rise of Nazi Germany and Fascist Italy and their combination as Axis powers in alliance with Japan clearly proved the weakness of Britain and she could no longer play the role of the holder of the European balance of power. Within the British empire the nationalist movements in India, Egypt and Iraq undermined the imperial authority of Britain.

At the conclusion of the Second World War, the United States and the Soviet Union rose as the two super powers with the monopoly of nuclear weapons. The changed international situation proved that Britain was no longer a great power playing the role of a balance in European politics. The former colonies of Britain became independent. Britain was content to be a purely European power and shed her imperial responsibilities. The economic position of Britain also became weak for she lost her income from the overseas investments which were the main source of her economic strength in the nineteenth century. Recognising the weak position of Britain, Prime Minister Harold Wilson announced the government's policy of withdrawal from the east of Suez in 1968. Thus Pax Britannica was dead with the disappearance of the British empire. Britain could no longer play the role of the keeper of world peace, for the empire which gave her the strength disappeared after the Second World War.

Peace of America

Pax Americana is a contemporary international phenomenon and refers to the global role of the United States as a super-power since 1945. Though the concept has acquired a wider connotation in view of Americans effort to create the world in the democratic image, Pax Americana originally developed as a manifestation of American dominance of the western hemisphere. Its roots can be traced to the Monroe Doctrine (1823). President James Monroe of the United States announced the doctrine with a view to preventing the European intervention on behalf of Spain in the revolt of the Spanish. American colonies against Spanish rule.

Monroe Doctrine: its principles. It is the base of Pax Americana in the western hemisphere.

The Monroe Doctrine which was actually drafted by the Secretary of State, John Quincy Adams, maintained:

1. that the American continent had no territory for future European colonisation;
2. that there was an essentially different political system in the Americas from Europe;
3. that the United States would regard any attempt by European powers to extend their influence in

the American as dangerous to its peace and security; and

4. that the united States would not interfere with existing European colonies nor participate in purely European wars.

The Doctrine remained the basis of American foreign policy for over a century but was modified subsequently. For example, President Theodore Roosevelt announced in 1904 that the U.S.A. was "an international police power" for the American continent. Thus the Monroe Doctrine expressed the objectives of Pax American. There should be no colonial system in the New World. The New World should be protected from, the evil consequences of the European power politics No European power should attempt to establish colonies in the New World.

Until 1945 Pax Americana was confined to the western hermisphere and it expressed the American dominance of the Latin American countries of South and Central America. Pax Americana also meant the exclusion of European powers from interfering in the affairs of the New World. Pax American differed from Pax Britannica for the Americans like the British, did not conquer the peoples of Asia and Africa and impose the colonial rule on them. They themselves developed an anti-colonial sentiment. The dollar diplomacy formed part and parcel of Pax Americana in Latin America. For the Latin Americans this meant American economic and cultural domination of their life.

The policy of isolationism was the concomitant of Pax Americana until 1945. Pax Americana enabled the U.S.A. to exert her economic sway over Latin America.

The Monroe Doctrine merely reiterated the Farewell Message of President George Washington that the United States should not get entangled in the politics and wars of Europe. In order to maintain peace in the western hemisphere, the United States should adhere to a policy of isolationism. She should concentrate on the development of her internal strength and stability and the best way to achieve this objective was not to get entangled in European politics. Only when American interests were seriously menaced, or the country's defence was in grave jeopardy, the United States should intervene in the affairs of Europe, with a view to protecting the nation's interest and security. This policy America followed since the promulgation of the Monroe Doctrine and intervened in the affairs of Europe on two occasions, first, at the time of the First World War and, second, at the time of the Second World War.

Pax Americana, until the beginning of the Second World War, meant that the United States should keep the New World in political isolation and away from the impact of the European power politics. The pursuit of such a policy of isolationism benefited the United States economically and brought her political gains. In the New World, the U.S.A. was the only advanced industrial country and possessed political stability. On the contrary, the Latin American countries were economically backward and politically unstable. Hence America was able to maintain her economic domination over Latin America. In fact, Pax Americana in the western hemisphere enabled the United States to impose a form of economic imperialism over Latin America.

Pax Americana since 1945: The United States did not withdraw from Europe in 1945 after the Axis power were defeated, she did after the First World War. For in Europe, Great Britain, the traditional holder of the balance of power lost her great power status and became militarily weak and exhausted. In Eastern Europe the state became communist and came under the influence of Soviet Russia. Finally, Soviet Russia became a super power possessing enormous superiority in conventional weapons. The West European nations, weak and exhausted and possessing a shattered economy were unable to resist Soviet penetration. The fall of democratic Czechoslovakia into the Communist orbit indicated the weakness of the Western nations. So the United States decided to stay in Europe and aid the West Europe nations in their economic recovery and political stability. Being a super power, the United States now thought of Pax Americana in global terms. She now faced another super power, in the Soviet Union whose universalistic nationalism tinged with Marxism was opposed to her own universalist nationalism inspired by democratic ideals. The contest between the two super-powers was at another level, the contest between the two different kinds of universalistic nationalism. It was an ideological contest between the two superpowers for the mastery over the mind of man. In the decision-making process, Pax Americana became Truman's doctrine of the containment of communism. President Truman helped Greece to combat successfully the growing menace of communism and launched the Marshall Plan (the European Recovery Programme) to check the growing influence of communism in West Europe. The whole anti-Communist policy was militarily consolidated when the NATO (the North Atlantic Treaty Organisation) was formed. When America realised that German unity could not be achieved, the Federal Republic of Germany was rehabilitated and became a member of the NATO. The anti-Communist ring was formed by extending the defensive alliances from the Middle East to Southeast Asia. The CENTO (Central Treaty Organisation) and the SEATO (Southeast Asia Treaty Organisation) revealed the American determination to contain communism.

In its relations with the Latin American states, the U.S.A. followed what Theodore Roosevelt described in 1940s as "an international police power". In order to pacify the growing discontent among the Latin American states and to create cooperative and harmonious inter-American relations, the United States concluded the Inter-American Treaty of Reciprocal Assistance with the Latin American states in 1947. The treaty provided that the member states should consider an attack against any American state as an attack against them collectively. America's aim was to isolate the New World, especially the unstable Latin Americana states, from Communist influence and subversion. Pax American could not achieve this objective. Communist threat to the western hemisphere increased and Cuba, under Fidel Castro, became communist. In order to check the growing influence of the Communists, the United States intervened in Guatemala and Nicaragua. The Cuban Missile crisis of 1962 was the consequence of the building of missile bases in Cuba by the Soviet Union.

In Southeast Asia, too, Pax Americana failed. After the French left Indo-China, the United States intervened in Vietnam but failed to check the advance of Communist forces under Ho Chi Minh and was finally compelled to withdraw from Vietnam. In East Asia earlier, the U.S.A. failed to check the rise of communism in China under Mao-Ze-Dong. China became a Communist country. However, the United States succeeded in building up Taiwan as an independent state. She had to agree to China's becoming a member of U.N. and a permanent member of the security council. The only success USA achieved in her anti-communist crusade was in Korea.

Return of Pax Americana: Between Thomas Jefferson and George Bush the USA has moved from a nation from within to a nation with manifest destiny about which presidents in the US has often spoken. Manifest Destiny began with the Americans wanting to get into the Pacific and Latin America. If Thomas Jefferson wanted to keep the USA off the European politics and if President McKinley intervened in Cuba and the Phillipines it was in both cases to safeguard their country's domestic interests as well as to extend them to the regions of the world so that they could get round it both form the west and the east. They came to Japan and right upto kamchatk (in the 2nd world war). They proposed to come to the Indian Ocean by the beginning of the 21st century. This was the vision that was articulated by Alfred Thayer Mahan. First the Atlantic and the Pacific were to be the protective shields for them. With Mahan these were extended and the frontiers of the Pacific and the Atlantic were extended to meet the challenge of a land power. The game of geopolitics was on. The spokesmen of geopolitics were Mackinder in Germany and Spykman in the US who refined the concept of sea power to include the Pacific rim. At the time when the concepts were being refined either the doctrines had been already practised or domestic politics of the country that was to be the target of the sea power concept was different. Mahan wrote exactly after a full century of British practice. Manifest destiny was practised as an extension of the power that had accrued to the US after it had become "indestructible union of indestructible states'. Also when the Mahan vision was articulated there was hardly any ideological foe in the main land Europe since before the revolution. President Wilson wanted to align himself with the Russians in the European game as today the changes in the post Soviet Union phase warrant US-CIS cooperation and the Chinese along with the most in the rest of the world talk not about manifest destiny but on the return of the American 'hegemony'.

It is only a couple of years ago that Francis Fukuyama took the pen up to say that the present century was one of victor of the liberal idea. This is true and not so accurate. It is the not so accurate description of the 20th century because it is in this century that many countries had moved out of the liberal idea and tried different paths of development in the erstwhile USSR, East Europe, some countries of Asia, Africa and Latin America. It is true in the sense that most of these countries have abandoned that path and returned to the fold with a few exceptions like the Chinese and the large countries like India. In the latter case the liberal ideas of democracy and enterprise were retained.

In case of China, despite the socialist rhetoric, the four modernisations involved selective opening up to the market and repressive political regime. In India there is a further accent on the play of the market forces and emphasis on the philosophy of macro economics. The crowning of the liberal idea comes from the collapse of the socialist experiment and the transition of the East European countries to market oriented economies and the non Communist democratic regimes under leaders that have for decades been regarded as dissentors by the communists—e.g. Havel in Czechosolovakia or Walesa in Poland. Infact the turn around to the liberal ideas for which the West has stood for considerable time with unbelievable tenacity only have made people develop a sense to immutability and eternity in the liberal idea. Two basic principles have dominated the changes that have reversed the developments after the Second World War. These are the ideas of self determination that President Wilson had introduced and the idea of human rights that became a talking point both with presidents Carter and Reagan.

Infact the latter became the part of the Helsinki basket of ideas and now every Slavo. Turkish leader and the leaders of the developing countries have to talk about it. Recently when Narasimha Rao attended the Commonwealth summit, he did not ignore the issue and of course emphasized the perspectives of development as far as the developing countries are concerned. The economic level also indicates that the competition between the two systems ended and has replaced a more benign competition among the three centres of power i.e. USA, Europe and Japan. At the economic level two things need to be kept in mind: (1) there has been an increase in the area of the international market and (2) the transnationalisation of the economies in which the western policies, particularly those of the international agencies are being governed by the needs of the developed countries in which the USA is still the dominant military and technological leader. This is not to deny that the competition among them over markets and policies towards specific countries in missing. It is very much there. For the Germans the aiding of the erstwhile Soviet Union was as significant an issue as the Japanese thought it was for them to aid the Chinese despite the fact the human rights record of the Chinese in the Tinnenmen square was a bone of contention between the western countries and the Japanese. Despite the fact that the Americans called for the food aid to the erstwhile Soviet Union the Japanese were not interested in giving any significant aid to them since they had the problem over the Kurile Islands.

At the military level the USA really gained and one can really speak about the return of Pax American. Gone are the days of the defeat in the Vietnam war and the Vietnam syndrome in which the Americans never had the courage to commit their forces for long periods in any part of the world there after. Gone are also the days of the Carter fiasco in the release of the hostages that the Iranians had. Gone are also the days when socialist oriented countries were getting liberated one after the other in Africa Asia and Latin America. The declaration of the SDI, the domination of the Honduras, the reversal in Nicaragua and Haiti brought about change in the international scene and came the Weinburger doctrine of short successful wars as a result of the new power of flexing of the American muscle. The new thinking of Gorbachev, the internal burgeoning Soviet crisis, the return of the Soviets to the negotiating table over the INF, the singing of the INF, CFE and START showed that the Soviet power was on the decline. Only later the events showed that the decline transformed into demise rather fast over the question of self determination.

The result of the changes in the soviet policies in the military sphere and their attitude to Eastern Europe added to the making of USA a supreme super power. In his latest message to the American President Bush has spoken of remaining where the nation has arrived, that is at the supreme position. This point the USA has acquired for reasons that have had a lot to do with the collapse of the Soviet Union than to the gaining of the intrinsic power that no one can possibly acquire overnight. The process of sovereignisation that has taken place in the erstwhile Union Republic is less a recognition of Lenin's theory of self-determination and more a result of the ideas of Wilson on self determination. The self-determination as practiced in the Soviet Union led to cultural autonomy and to central command economy, political control and accompanying side effects. The festering fights over enclaves of freedom and independence are only some of the other features of the malaise that expressed itself in the struggle for autonomy that the Baltics have and that the Georgians are still so vehemently protecting. Even the Russian republic is facing the problem since the various peoples that are the inhabitants of the region are claiming national specifities in their economy and polity despite the fact that there are attempts by the post—Soviet leadership to achieve a modicum of unity through the formation of the commonwealth of Independent States. The process of self determination has a strategic and tactical angle to it. The assertion of the Ukrainians, Belarus, the Russians, Georgians and the other republics over the armed forces is removing the sting from the prowess of the Red Army. It appears that the decline of Red Army so assiduously built by Trotsky onwards is as fast as it is in case of the Army that was built by the Czar. The Czarist Army had collapsed after six months of the revolution. The present Defence minister given the task of reforming the Army of whatever is left of it after the move of nation formations, wants two years in the ensuring turmoil to reform the Army, while the Officer's assemblies from the grassroots level to the top have been wanting to preserve the organisation. This threat to the US power no longer exists and is only an added factor, the return of Pax Americana after the half war that the Allies won in the Gulf against Saddam Hussein. From the Korean war in the fifties to the Gulf war of the 90s the UN and the US had seen many ups and downs but the principle of collective security was asserted under the US leadership. The air war, the Patriot missile replaced the earlier instruments of war but heralded the return of the Pax Americana that had touched its nadir in Vietnam. The added advantage was that this time the US came as the head of the Judea—Christian World. As such it has been able to play a decisive role even in the peace process that has dogged the West Asian peace process since the end of the Second World War.

The diplomacy of James Baker from Madrid to Moscow to Washington only shows that the USA controls the levers of the Israeli economy to bring them to the negotiating table as it does manipulate the Syrians, Egyptians and the Jordanians and the inhabitants of Palestine with or without PLO.

Some caveats however need to be added to the return of the Pax Americana. At the technological level the war between Japan, Europe and America in the coming century is going to be as difficult as the trade war between Japan and the USA. At the political level the possibilities of fragmentation inside and outside USA should not be under estimated even if currently it is being felt in the curve from the Balkans to the Middle East through Eurasia. At the economic level the USA itself may have to cut on its own defence budgets on projects of the Navy, new weapons procurement strategies, SDI etc. precisely because of economic and strategic reasons. At the societal level the prevalent violence and its contingent dangers brought out by the racial riots in the Los Angeles combined with the dangers of the drug menance and illiteracy may show the agenda that may worry George Bush into the next elections.

Pax Americana does not only suggest a military clout, a victory of Mr. X's containment, it also implies upholding of some philosophical ideas and strategic orthodoxies like non-proliferation of nuclear weapons regime that is sought to be used to perforate South Asia.

Peace of the Soviet Union

Peace of Soviet Russia was also a manifestation of the nationalistic universalism promoed by undivided Soviet Union which was the first communist state founded by Lenin on the principles of Marxism and creatively interpreted by him. During the inter-war priod (1919-1939), Soviet Russia which was mainly preoccupied with rapid economic development on Marxist lines and with the maintenance of internal stability could not play an important role in affairs. After the Second World War in which her role in defeating Nazi Germany was significant and decisive, soviet Russia became a super power rivalling the United States in nuclear strength. Stalin's great achievement was the building up of buffer communist states in Eastern Europe between the U.S.S.R. and the Western powers and the permanent dismemberment of a powerful, united Germany by turning Eastern Germany into a Communist state. The whole of East Europe came under the Russian sphere of influence and a solid bloc of allies firmly united by ideology came into existence. The Pan-slavism of the Czarist Russia which could not succeed was transformed into Pax Sovietica of Communist Russia which could expand into central Europe from the solid base of Eastern Europe. The Communist states of Eastern Europe were the first countries to come under Pax Sovietica.

The U.S.S.R. was the first Communist state and it became the model of other Communist states. The principles and practice of Soviet Russia, which were first developed by Lenin and later continued by Stalin, guided the founding of the communist states in Eastern Europe. In short, Soviet Russia became the Mecca of the Marxist world. This primacy was challenged by the Chinese Communists and, by the Yugoslav Communists led by Marshal Tito.

Pax Sovietica need to be interpreted in terms of the Marxist ideology. In practical terms it meant the extension of Soviet influence, first, to West Europe and, later, to the other parts of the world. It was a theoretical necessity From the Communist point of view. According to Marxism-Leninism, the official orthodoxy of the Soviet Union, there can be no lasting peace between the capitalist and Communist Countries. Peace is possible only when the exploiting capitalist countries become Communist by means of a violent proletarian revolution. Thus from the Marxist theoretical point of view Pax Sivietica aimed at international peace by eliminating capitalism, the source of conflict.

In practical terms, Pax Sovietica was linked with the national interest of Soviet Russia. It meant the support of Russia by the Communist of other nations.

Pax Sovietica, apart from its theoretical implications, had practical import. It was inked with the national interest of Soviet Russia. The safety of the Communist states other than Russia, depended on the strength and power of the Soviet Union. So they must support the U.S.S.R. in her struggles against the capitalist countries. International affairs they must follow the line of Soviet foreign policy. Pax Sovietica meant that peace is possible only when the other Communist countries lined up with the Soviet Union. In other words, the interest of Soviet Russia as the interest of world communist movement was the assumption behind the argument we that in supporting the policies of the

Soviet Russia, the Communist countries and the leftist forces in democratic countries would promote the cause of world communism.

"A Communist country has no option to give up its Communist way of life. Soviet Union has the right to intervene and restore communism." The case of Hungary (1958).

Soviet statesmen and thinkers interpreted Pax Sovietica as the maintenance of Russian dominance over the Soviet bloc in Europe. Just as the United States maintained its predominant position in Latin America through the Organisation American State (OAS), so the Soviet Union maintained her supreme position in East Europe through the Warsaw Pact. Just as the United States wanted to contain communism in the western hemisphere and exercised the right to intervene in the internal affairs of any Latin American states, such as Nicaragua and Gautemala, to put down Communist influence, so Soviet Russia 'contained' the growth of the liberal democratic spirit in Eastern Europe and exercised the right to intervene in the internal affairs of any Communist state, such as Hungary and Czechoslovakia to put down the rise of bourgeois tendencies. Khrushchev interpreted Pax Sovietica as preservation of Communism in East Europe and the maintenance of Soviet dominance over the Communist countries in East Europe.

Thus Pax Sovietica meant the extension of the then Soviet influence and power over Eastern Europe by the establishment of sympathetic Communist states. The opportunity came, when the former Soviet Union drove out the Nazi German forces occupying Eastern Europe during the Second World War. In the course of the invasion of Germany from the eat, Russia conquered East European countries and imposed communist regimes over them. Thus East Germany, Hungery, Rumania, Bulgaria, Yogoslavia and Poland became Communist and came under Soviet influence. The democratic regime in Czechoslovakia was overthrown and that country became communist.

The Second World War ended in 1945 without a general peace settlement, because of the differences of vital interests between the United State and the former Soviet Union, both of which reached the new international status of super powers. The Cold War began in 1945 between the two super powers and the Americans decided to stay in Europe and to arrest the further penetration of communism into western Europe. In order to safeguard her interests, the former soviet Union began to tighten her control over Eastern Europe. Two multilateral treaties, one economic and other military, were concluded between the Soviet Union and her East European Communist allies. The economic agreement led to the establishment of the COMECON (the Council for Mutual Economic Assistance and the military and defence agreement led to the establishment of the Warshaw pact (1955).

The Soviet Union emerged as the undisputed powerful leader of the Eaat European Communist countries. Pax Sovietica was established over Eastern Europe. However, Russia had to face two challenges to her leadership. Yugoslavia under Marshal Josef tito broke away from the Soviet bloc owing to ideological reason and soon became one of the founder members of the Non-aligned Movement (NAM) along with India and Egypt. Similarly, Albania also left the Soviet bloc and sided with China in the Sino-Soviet rift. A further erosion of Soviet influence in Asia occurred, when Communist China became the leading Asian power and developed differences with undivided Russia. China began to compete with Russia for the leadership of the Communist movement.

The "Middle Kingdom" Complex of China

The Historical roots of the complex: Today, China which

has become one of the five members of the excusive nuclear club is a great Asian power competing with the Soviet Union for the leadership of the communist world. But in the nineteenth century, in spite of the weak and disintegrating rule of the Manchu dynasty. China, unlike in other parts of Asia excluding Japan, was not conquered and colonised by the Western powers, though the western powers whom the Chinese called "ocean devils" humiliated China by imposing on her unequal treaties. Apart form India, China is the only region where an ancient tradition has flourished and persisted down to the modern times.

We have to examine the historical roots of the "Middle kingdom" complex of modern China, which influences her conduct of foreign policy. The traditional belief of the Chinese has been that they live at the centre of the world, though it is false from the geographical point of view. But for a very long period the Chinese believed it to be true. C.P. Fitzgerald in his book, The Chinese View of Their Place in the World, observes, "They (Chinese) did indeed live in a closed world, of which fertile China was the centre; to the north the barren steppe, to the east the endless sea, to the west the highest mountain system in the world, southward tropical jungles. In their favoured environment they developed a civilization which owed very little to contact with any foreign people, and had no links with any people of a similar level of development."

The ancient Chinese distinguished between the civilised and barbarian peoples. During the period of Central Kingdom, the Chinese called themselves as Hsias, linked by culture and language but remaining politically independent. The northern nomadic people living in the steppes beyond China were described variously as Jung. Ti and Hu. The southern forest dwellers who were also rice cultivators, like the Chinese were called Man. The southern people were absorbed into the Chinese culture, they became Chinese and were admitted into the circle of civilized states. But the northern nomads who lived in the steppes were beyond the pale of the Chinese civilisation. To prevent the nomads from raiding into China, the Chinese rulers began constructing long wall along the ridges of the mountain chain separating north China from the Mongolian steppe. Later these walls were linked to form the great Wall of China running from the sea coast for fourteen hundred miles to the borders of the Central Asian desert. The Great Wall symbolises the physical limit set to the bounds of civilisation by the ancient Chinese.

Thus the Chinese possessed a sense of unity and a belonging to a civilisation rather than to a state or a nation from the very early times. "It (the sense of unity) transcended political allegiances and the strife of princes. It formed, in later times, the foundation for the acceptance by the Chinese peoples as a whole of the firm, strong and enduring centralised government which first united the country in the third century B.C." This is the historical legacy inherited by the modern Chinese Communists who still continue the tradition of centralised administration.

The absence of any rival centre of civilisation was a factory which contributed most powerfully to the traditional Chinese view of the world. During the period of the T'ang dynasty (A.D. 618-907), China was consolidated into a new centralised empire. The T' and period is of fundamental importance since from that time onwards the Chinese world outlook was so firmly established that it did not subsequently change until modern times. From the T'ang perid onwards the unity of China persisted. The Chinese regarded the ideals of the unified empire as normal and right, because they were based on traditional Chinese concepts which made the empire the synonym of the civilised world and treated all beyond China as barbarian. Under the T'ang dynasty the penetration of the south continued until all the modern territory of the Chinese state had been colonised and absorbed into the empire except the present province of Yunnan.

Thus the T'ang period was a turning-point in Chinese history. It fixed the Chinese world outlook which did not alter until modern times. Rather more than one thousand years ago, the T'ang dynasty fixed the geographical limits in which the Chinese people were to live until modern times. T'ang China had much wider contact with West Asia and East Europe (Byzantinum) than China had before. Yet these contacts with foreigners did not make any deep impression upon their sense of superiority. Their view of China as being the centre of the world remained unshaken. The foreign residents, servants, merchants and pilgrims served a useful purpose but they certainly held no position of equality. To the Chinese of the T'ang period it was evident that "they lived in the most advanced community of which they had knowledge, and the further contacts with distant states confirmed them in this belief."

C.P. Fitzgerald observes that the Chinese attitude towards foreigners was determined by their experience with the Monogolian nomads whom they regarded as barbarians. The experience of the T'ang thus powerfully reinforced the Chinese belief in their own superiority, and in the relative-or absolute barbarism of other peoples. With the exception of the distance countries of western Asia, mainly known through their merchants, the only civilised peoples were those such as the Korans and Japanese who had adopted, Chinese culture and remodelled their own institutions in the image of China. The foreigners best to the Chinese were the nomads of the Mongolian Steppe, at this period the Turks."

The Mongols had been superior in military matters, but in these alone; the evident superiority of the Europeans in this respect, therefore, did not impress the Chinese as proof of cultural equality but rather tended to show them in an unfavourable light.

Supporting the nationalists while the Soviet Union had no interest to support the Communists in China as it feared that a war would disturb the equilibrium between the post-war power blocs.

In such conditions Mao devised the theory of Middle kingdom concept or intermediate zone. This was further elaborated in his "World's Eye view from a Yenan cave. According to this theory, China attacked USA as trying to establish its dominance over the world. Under the guise of an impending war with Soviet Union USA was creating a global network of bases like SEATO, NATO, CENTO. US policy was actually directed at the countries with which it had form regional pacts. As such Mao called upon all the democratic forces which found themselves in contradiction with the USA should join hands to form a united front against it.

For the implementation of the 'Middle kingdom' concept, China made great efforts to improve its economic and military strength so that it could play an important role in world affairs. Besides this, China projected an image as the supporter of nationalist movements anywhere in the world. In 1964, during the period of Sino-Soviet conflict, Mao viewed that there were two intermediate zones in the world. Asia, Africa and Latin America constitute the first intermediate zone while Europe. North America and Oceanic constituted the second. The two superpowers. Soviet revisionism and US imperialism were trying to sandwitch other countries of the world. The countries of the intermediate zones are subjected to control, intervention and bullying by the two superpowers.

The Chinese historical tradition which influenced the Chinese foreign policy in the past was that China did not rely upon, or except assistance from, foreign powers. During the they day of the empire foreign policy was determined by the relations between the empire and the local rulers. The local rulers paid tribute and recognised the supremacy of China and its Emperor, the Son of Heaven. The imperial Chinese never dealt with allies but they had dealings with their vassals. The status of the outsiders who were always regarded as inferior vassals carried with its the traditional belief of the Chinese that their land was at the centre of the world. The Chinese world-picture was not as international system of equal sovereign states. The Chinese thought that their land was an oasis of civilisation surrounded by a desert of barbarian kingdoms, such as Burma which paid tributes.

The present leaders of Communist China are not Confucians but they have been influenced by the history and tradition of their culture and one can discover similarities between the Confucian thought and the Maoist doctrine. The idea of the duty to educate the people in wisdom and virtue now epitomised in the "thought of Mao Ze-doing" has its parallel in Confucianism. Communist China's approach to foreign relations reinforces her traditional view of the world, which sees China as the centre, the sole upholder of true civilisation and the law-giver to the barbarians. C.P. Fitzgerald says, "there can be no doubt that this view, in a modern form, is prevent in China and is positively stated in the many polemical articles which have appeared since the dispute with the Soviet Union has come into the open. The Chinese now claim to be the upholders to pure Marxism, and denounce Russia as faint-hearted 'revisions", and too ready, for fear of nuclear war, to betray world revolution in vavour of a form of co-existence which in reality would lead to the perpetuation of the capitalist society. China, on the contrary, is not afraid of the "paper tigers" of imperialism, is ready to step in and support revolutionary wars...She has also the courage, the true doctrine, and will therefore get the support of the working-class of the whole world, and is thus Test fitted for the leadership of the future world Communist society."

The Chinese view of the world has not fundamentally changed. But it has been adjusted to the imperative needs of the modern world in which Western political thought and technology have been dominant. This adjustment has been made only with a view to enabling China to occupy the central place still. To do this the Chinese communists have found it necessary to accept from the West a new doctrine to replace the inadequate Confucian teaching. They have discovered in communism, or Marxism-Leninism, a doctrine more easily assimilable to Chinese ways. Though the Chinese leaders have accepted communism, they can not for long, acknowledge their debt to the West and accept the humble position of a pupil. "Mao Tse-Tung had to enrich the treasury Marxist-Leninist thought so that the contents of that treasury could become current coin in China; it was inevitable that Chinese Marxism should be found to be purer than that of Russia, that Mao should be hailed as the greater prophet, and that 'some people' should be shown to be in Error.

Peace and International Understanding

The most important achievement of India's foreign policy has been its valuable contribution towards the promotion of world peace and international understanding. India stands for maintenance of peace in the world through the United Nations. India has always endeavoured for the peaceful settlement of international disputes and has never been an aggressor against any country. India's faith in humanity has been the basis of its international relations. It is also the signatory to all the major Human Rights documents of he UN. Being one of the founder members of the UN. Being one of the founder members of the UN, India has been deeply involved in the various UN activities, particularly in peacekeeping operations.

Disarmament

There can be no lasting peace without disarmament. India's foreign policy has strongly been in favour of disarmament with highest priority to total nuclear disarmament. An 'Action Plan for Nuclear Weapon Free and Non-Violent World Order' was presented by India in 1988 in the 3rd session of the UN General Assembly devoted to disarmament. India has always been seriously concerned about the nuclear arms race. It has been vehemently opposing the nuclear Non-Proliferation Treaty and Comprehensive Nuclear Test ban Treaty due to their discriminatory nature. India has been adaminant not to give up its nuclear option until all other countries do so.

Regional Cooperation

An important aspect of India's foreign policy has been to promote regional cooperation among South Asian countries. Attempts have been made in various other parts of the world to promote peace and cooperation amongst states through the formation of regional organizational. Some notable examples are Association of South East Asian Nations, European Economic cooperation Organization of African Unity. India has always believed in peace and cooperation with all its neighbours. Thus, seven countries of south Asia namely India, Pakistan, Sri Lana, Bangladesh. Maldives, Nepal and Bhutan joined together to form the South Asian Association for Regional cooperation. The idea of South Asian Regional Cooperation was first mooted by the President of Bangladesh. Zia-ur-Rehman. between 1977 and 1980, he visited Nepal, India, Pakistan and Sri Lanka for consultation with the leaders of these countries in order to give concrete shape to the idea. These initiatives resulted in the formation of SAARC in 1985. During the first South Asian Summit held in December 1985 at Dhaka, the heads of the seven founding member states adopted the charter of SAARC. The main objectives of SAARC are to promote welfare and to improve the quality of life of the People of South Asia, to accelerate social and economic growth of the region, to foster collective self-alliance, to strengthen cooperation among South Asian countries and to collaborate in the economic, social, cultural, technical and scientific fields. India is the biggest member state among SAARC countries. It has a huge economy, territory, population and developmental base in comparison to the other members. This makes the role of India important in the functioning and growth of SAARC. India also values SAARC as complementary to its bilateral relationship with its south Asian neighbouring countries. But the bilateral disputes and tensions between India and Pakistan and the apprehensions about India's hegemony by some other neighbours affect the strength and effectiveness of the SAARC. The political will and direction by the member states can only make SAARC effective and strong. There is a need for more sociocultural exchanges and cooperation among SAARC countries.

Foreign Policy and Its Determinants

This involvement must be systematic and based on some well-defined principles. The principles and the purpose of a state is reflected in the foreign policy. The importance of the foreign policy has been highlighted by scholars in various ways. According to one scholar, a state without a foreign policy is like a ship without a radar which drifts a aimlessly without any direction by every storm and sweep of events. According to Prof. Taylor "Foreign Policy of a sort will go on so long as there are sovereign states."

Meaning of Foreign Policy

There is no unanimity amongst scholars regarding the meaning of foreign policy and various definitions have been offered. According to Padelford and Lincoln. "A state's foreign policy is the totality of its dealings with the external environment. Foreign policy is more than a collection of official documents, formal records of actions and public statements. A foreign policy statement can be simple and succinct...or it may be complicated and imprecise ...Policy is the overall result of the process by which a state translates it broadly conceived goals and interests into specific courses of action in order to achieve its objectives and preserve its interests."[1]

Prof. F.S. Northedge says that foreign policy implies "the use of political influence in order to induce other states to exercise their law making power in a manner desired by the state concerned; it is an interaction between forces originating outside the country's borders and those working within them."

Prof. Joseph Frankel says that "foreign policy consists of decisions and actions which involves to some appreciable extent relations between one state and others."[2] Hugh Gibson defines foreign policy as "a well-rounded comprehensive plan based on knowledge and experience for conducting the business of government with the rest of the world. It is aimed at promoting and protecting the interests of the nations. This calls for a clear understanding of what those interests are and how far we can hope to go with the means at our disposal. Anything less than this falls short of being a foreign policy."[3]

George Modelski says that foreign policy is "the system of activities evolved by communities for changing the behaviour of other states and for adjusting their own activities to the international environment."[4]

The Brookings Institution in its book *Major Problems of United States Foreign Policy 1952-3*, used the term foreign policy to refer to the complex and dynamic political course that a nation follows in relation to other states. According to it foreign policy of a nation is more than the sum total of its foreign policy (thought out courses of action for achieving objectives), for it also includes its commitment, the current forms of its *interests* and *objectives* and the principles of right conduct that it professes.

A perusal of the above definitions of foreign policy shows that scholars have laid emphasises either on the plan of action or policy as executed. However, they all agree that the foreign policy is concerned with the behaviour of a state towards other states.

Determinants of Foreign Policy Factors (Factors Influencing Foreign Policy)

The foreign policy of a country is influenced by so many factors that it is not possible to enumerate all of them here. Some of the important factors which influence the foreign policy of a country or constitute the inputs of the foreign policy are given hereunder. Broadly speaking these factors fall into two categories viz. internal and external.

Internal Factors

Size. In the first place the size of a state's territory as well as its population greatly influences its foreign policy. Generally the leaders and people of countries with small territory and population do not expect their country to carry great weight in international affairs. On the other hand the leaders and people of large countries are ready to assume special responsibilities. However, sometime even small states which have rich resources also leave a deep impact on world politics. For example, the oil-rich countries of Middle East, though small in size, are playing significant role in the international politics. Likewise if a country possesses large territory which is barren and a population which is unskilled, it may not be able to play any effective role in international politics.

Geography. The geography of a country, including its fertility, climate, location in relation to other land masses, and water-ways etc. also influence the country's foreign policy. It is a major factor in determining self-sufficiency of a country. Generally land-locked countries, nations in the tropics and those bordering a super-power are less self-sufficient in comparison to the countries which have access to warm-water ports or are located in the temperate zones and far removed from super powers. For example in the nineteenth century USA adopted isolationist policy chiefly on account of its geographical location. Though the importance of geographic factors is acknowledged almost at all hands, its importance has considerably declined due to technological and scientific developments. For example, due to improvement in the means of transport and communication the world has greatly shrunk and the perception of large bodies of water as natural barriers to military attack has greatly diminished. But still geographical location of a country has a deep impact on the determination of its foreign policy. India adopted policy of non-alignment because of geographical location. The presence of two major powers on its borders (USSR and China) deterred it from joining power blocs.

Culture and History. The cultural and historical traditions of a country also deeply influence the foreign policy. Generally people possessing a unified common culture and historical experience can pursue an effective foreign policy because of the support of all sections of society who share the same values and memories. On the other hand, a country which is culturally and historically fragmented cannot pursue an equally effective foreign policy. According to Prof. Rosenau "the influence of cultural factors is not limited to the impact of societal unity upon the formulation and implementation of foreign policy. Equally important are the processes through which the contents of shared norms and practices of society, as distinguished from the degree of unity that supports them, shape the plans that are made and the activities that are undertaken with respect to the external world."[5]

Economic Development. The stage of economic development which a country has attained also has its impact on its foreign policy. Generally the industrially advanced countries feel more deeply involved in relations with other countries because they have to import different kinds of raw materials and commodities from other countries. They are also in the look out of latest knowledge and technical know-how. Therefore they maintain intimate trade relations with their trading partners. All this leads to intimate links between the groups and people of one country with their counterparts in the other country. Again, an industrial country is expected to have a higher gross national product (GNP) and can devote greater funds for external purposes viz. economic aid programme military ventures and extensive diplomatic commits. On the other hand, industrially backward countries are not able to actively involve themselves in external affairs. The lack of scientists, engineers and other specialists in the country prevents them from taking advantage of the technological break through abroad.

Technology. Advancement in technology, which effects the military and economic capabilities of a state, also exercises profound influence on the foreign policy. However, this factor influences the foreign policy only in an indirect manner viz. by influencing other sources of foreign policy.

Social Structure. The social structure of a society also exercises profound influence on its foreign policy. A society which is sharply divided on the basis of wealth, religion, regional imbalances etc. cannot pursue effective foreign policy on account of division and lack of co-operation among various groups. On the other hand a homogeneous society possessing strong sense of national unity can pursue a more effective foreign policy. It is well known the Britain stood as one person under the leadership of Churchill during the second world war and the people gladly suffered all kinds of hardships to preserve their unity because of social solidarity. No doubt, it is not easy to trace the impact of social structure on the foreign policy plans and behaviour, because of the involved subtleties, but no student of foreign policy can "afford to ignore the external consequences of the internal social structure and of the slow changes it may be undergoing."[6]

Public Mood. Public mood is another important determinant of a country's foreign policy. Though it is generally held that the public mood usually follows rather than guides the foreign policy making process, it can exercise lot of influence on the determination of foreign policy if basic realignment in the prevailing great power structure takes place and the state becomes more involved or more isolated from the world affairs. It may be noted that generally in an authoritarian system the public mood does not influence the foreign policy, but in a democratic system based on political accountability considerable weight has to be accorded to the changing public mood and sentiments.

Political Organisation. The political organisation found in a country also greatly influences the foreign policy. Generally under authoritarian systems quick foreign policy decisions are possible because the decision making power rests with an individual assisted by his clique. But as the leaders under this system are isolated from the operational environments and the subordinate policy makers provide the information which is perceived by the superiors, there is every possibility of a discrepancy between the psychological and operational aspects of the foreign policy. Further, under this system undesirable opposition can be suppressed through censorship and promulgation of regulations. On the other hand in a country possessing a democratic structure the citizens can freely express their opinion on the domestic as well as foreign policy which naturally leaves its impact on the foreign policy of the country. Under democratic system there is very little discrepancy between what the officials want to believe about the state of world politics and the actual position because the subordinate policy makers make available critical and detached information.

Within the democratic system itself the difference in political structure has its impact or foreign policy. For example, under a parliamentary system of government based on co-operation between the Legislature and the Executive, the cordial relations between the two wings have an impact on country's foreign policy. On the other hand under Presidential system based on the principle of separation of powers, the relations between the two wings are likely to be more strained, which affects the ambiguity or continuity of foreign policy. Similarly, different foreign policy is likely to emerge under bi-party system and multi-party systems. Generally under bi-party system the government is likely to have a clear cut majority and conduct itself in a more decisive manner regarding the conduct of foreign relations. In contrast to this, under multi-party system conflicting view points and interests may have to be reconciled. This may lead either to the avoidance or postponment of the decision.

Role of Press. The press also plays a vital role in the foreign policy formulation process. The press contributes to this process by supplying factual information on the basis of which the people take decision; by publishing specialised articles on current international developments which enables the people to understand the significance of developments in their country in relation to the past developments; and by analysing the policy of the government in regard to foreign affairs. The press also plays an important role in publicizing the foreign policy of the country.

The role of the press however, depends on the political system prevailing in the country, the rate of literacy as well as the attitude of government.

Political Accountability. The nature of political accountability prevailing in a system also greatly influences the foreign policy of the country. Generally in an open political system, the demands of citizens and groups get articulated and transmitted to foreign policy formulators. The framers of foreign policy cannot ignore these demands. If fact quite often the policy formulators anticipate these demands while formulating the foreign policy. On the other hand under a closed system the public reactions are neither available nor given much importance.

Leadership. The leadership also plays a vital role in the shaping of a country's foreign policy. According to Rosenau "A leader's beliefs about the nature of international arena and the goals that ought to be pursued therein, his or her peculiar intellectual strengths and weaknesses for analysing information and making decisions, his or her past background and the extent of its relevance to the requirements of the role, his or her emotional needs and host of other personality traits—these are but a few of the idiosyncratic factors that can influence the planning and execution of foreign policy."[7] No doubt, the qualities of leadership have a deep impact on the country's foreign policy but their role is greatly constrained by the governmental and social structure. Further, the role of leadership is not identical in all countries. In less developed countries their role is greater as compared to industrialised societies. In industrialised societies the individuals enjoy very limited discretion in high governmental and non-governmental positions.

External Factors

In addition to the internal factors which influence a country's foreign policy discussed above, a number of external factors also exercise considerable influence on the foreign policy of a country. In our times the world has become so interlinked that incidents in other countries have their immediate impact on other countries. Thus a *coup d'etat* in a neighbouring country or nationalisation of oil companies in middle east or release of a proposed arms control agreements are events which influence the actions of leader in other countries.

7

International Economic Order

Generally, economic development of a country is measured on the basis of its national income and per capita income. National income is defined as the total value of all the goods and services produced within a country plus income coming from abroad. When the total national income is divided by the total population, it is called per capital income. Both these concepts are described in terms of money. Every country tries to raise its national income and per capital income with the available resources. For achieving a higher level of economic development, these two are essential requirements, but may not be sufficient. People have to be ensured a regular and higher income provided with basic amenities like food, clothing shelter, health and education.

Thus, economic development can be defined as long term increase in per capital income along with improvement in quality of life. The World is undergoing structural adaptation, reason being that the World Economy is continuing to grow slowly. Despite the success in reducing inflation, almost everywhere, expectations of faster growth have not been fulfilled. Since, the economic recovery that started in 1993, in no year has World output growth exceeded 3% per annum so far. The prospects of the same are for a continuation of this slow growth in the years to come also. A certain pattern of growth may be absерved in the Developing World since 1990, where growth has averaged 4.85% including China, and 3.9% if China is excluded. Much of this growth has been due to East Asia, where expansion has been both fast and stable.

International economics has for its field of study and practice the traffic in goods, services, gifts, capital and the precious metals as the ownership of these item changes from the residents of one country to these of another. It describes and analyses this traffic, as well as the laws, institutions and practices under which it operates. It draws inferences, develops tendencies and laws that condition the manner in which International transactions take place.

The principles and theories of International economics not only are consistent with the general body of economic theory, but are often a special application of these more general laws. International economics has a long and interesting history and arrived at its present state of development after a long journey of many years by trial and error method. The pattern of International economic relations has seldom remained stable for a long period, country after country has risen to importance in the field of International Trade.

Adam Smith in his book entitled "An Inquiry into the Nature and Causes of the Wealth of Nations", quoted that "What is prudence in the conduct of every private family, can scarce be folly in that of a great kingdom. If a foreign country can supply us with a commodity cheapter than we ourselves can make it, better buy it, than to produce it. Thus, Adam Smith in the late 1700's, characterised the advantages of individual and international specialisation.

The fundamental argument for international specialisation and exchange of goods and services rests on a theory popularised by David Ricardo (1772-1823). His analysis, later on is being called the principle of "Comparative costs", marked an advance ever Smith's for Ricardo reasoned that it might be advantageous for a nations to import an item even if it could be produced internally at a lower cost. Much of today's international economic theory represents either a modification or a refinement of the early principle.

The development of the principle of comparative advantage was furthered by John E. Cairnes (1832-1875). One of the problems where he directed his attention was the theory of value in domestic and international trade. Then, much of the success in modernising the foundations of international economic theory is attributed to Alfred Marshall (1892-1924). His meet famous work, *Principles of Economics,* represented an endeavour to improve upon and to synthesise the cost theories of the Classical School and utility theories of the Austrian or Psychological School. It is generally recognised that capital is a balancing item. While Sir Arthur Satler pointed out in 1880-1913 that Income on investment should be treated as a balancing item.

Further, modification of the principle of Comparative costs was provided by F.W. Taussing (1859-1940). He concluded that despite the unrealistic assumptions, their treatment of trade theory was approximately correct. Gottfried Haborler also endeavoured to improve the theory of trade by important shift in assumptions and analysis. Despite various efforts to bring the principle of comparative advantage class to reality, it remained subject to persistent criticism. One of the more constructive critics was Bortil Ohlin, who, in following an approach employed by Hockacher, introduced the mutual interdependence theory (1933). Ohlin's mutual interdependence theory received widespread acceptance. It not only provides and adequate and realistic explanation for the causes of trade but it is also a complete theory in the sense that all relevant variables are embodied in it.

Where the foreign demand for a country's exports is inelastic lower prices do not necessarily mean increased exports and a larger volume of money in circulation,but could result in lower exports and a smaller volume of money in circulation. Where balance of payments adjustments are not automatically made by changes in exchange rates or prices, there is a possibility that they will be so adjusted by means of changes in interests rates or income. Few International Economist are of the view that the reduction of nationalism and the abolition of all barriers to International Trade would place nations and all factors of production, wherever they are located, into competition with one another, with the result that there would be a levelling of the economies of all countries.

The arguments in favour of protection is based on keeping the money at home, to reduce unemployment, for equalisation of production costs, infant industry argument, cheap foreign labour, National security, diversification, etc.

Custom Simplification

The customs tariff is one of several obstacles which importers of foreign goods into the domestic country must meet. As the executive branch sought to reduce tariffs through the application of the Reciprocal Trade Agreements, the complexity of customs regulations, tariff rates, procedures, classifications, and valuations become increasingly apparent. These regulations constitute a sort of "invisible tariff" which effectively serve to confound exporters and importers alike and to impade the importation of goods into the other countries.

The Kennedy Round was 6th in the series of Trade negotiations. The GATT sponsored Kennedy Round which was one of the more important of the several negotiating sessions which have been undertaken. The completion of the negotiations in itself reflects a continued willingness on the part of most of the major trading nations to work toward the liberalisation of World Trade, particularly in industrial commodities.

No doubt, the effects of Regional and Cultural differences form part of the International Economics, they are often not as important owing to the effects of different acts of rules and regulations. Further, national laws also tend to isolate each nation from its neighbours, making a considerable difference in the way trade is conducted within a country and between countries. Moreover trade helps in efficient global allocation of resources.

International migration on a large scale is impracticable, but nations can improve their economic situations by exchanging goods and services. The central concept of the International trade theory has been of the "Comparative Advantage" of a trading nation.

We know that the Classical Economist were the champions of the cause of free trade. But during the great depression of 1930s the World saw how weak, it was, and how far away the Classical argument was away from the realities of everyday life. Trade in the modern World has became more and an exchange of industrial products among the rich countries. The exports of developing countries are still mainly consisted of raw materials and basic commodities with the slight opening for their manufactured exports increasingly threatened by a variety of factors tending to become more and more restrictive. Moreover, there was not a significant change in the trade policies of Developed Countries and the problems of Developing Countries were further aggravated as their trade failed to keep pace, on the other hand, richer countries recorded further increase in their Gross National Product and benefits of their affluence failed to penetrate the large number of developing countries. In 1964, the United Nations Conference on Trade and Development (UNCTAD) was established in December, 1964. Prior to this, International Trade problems were being considered primarily within the framework of GATT (1948).

The main purpose behind establishing the UNCTAD was to solve the problems of World Trade and Developments arising from the dissatisfactory working of the GATT. The idea of GSP emerged in the Second UNCTAD at Delhi in 1968 and the whole scheme of Generalised System of Preferences (GSP) was finalised in October, 1970. European Economic Community (EEC) was the first to implement the GSP in July, 1971. GSP in a significant departure from the trade pattern based in Most Favoured Nations clause and the principle of reciprocity. GSP was aimed at to bring about a better balance between the lending trading countries and their weak partners i.e. developing countries.

It is very important to bear in mind that the GSP markets are essentially "Buyers Markets" wherein suppliers from all over the World compets. The buyers, therefore, expect prompt and regular supplies strictly as per the approved samples, so as not to upset the commitments to their own customers. Only few countries could get the benefits during the period of more than a 26 years of its operation. Moreover, GSP is not a panacea for all the trade and development problems faced by the Developing Countries.

Thus, the old paradigm of comparative advantage vested for these countries having labour-intensive products and techniques alongwith the specific natural resources derived and soil-based products. Arthur Lewis postulated that Developing Countries having comparative advantage in labour-intensive products and in labour-intensive techniques, made possible because of unlimited surplus labour. But now, with modern technology and mobility of finance and capital these countries can obtain, and are obtaining comparative advantage in capital intensive and technology intensive products and services.

A significant development in 1996, 1997 and on the basis of estimated and expected figures for the year 1998, it has been observed that their is a slowdown in the World Trade. While, the World merchandise exports had grown at rates 3 to 4 times than that of World output in the previous 3 years upto 1997, the differences were much smaller and a tendency which can be expected to continue in the coming years, as the initial effects of widespread trade liberalisation and globalisation, particularly in Developing Countries, taper, off. This recent slowdown in World Trade has also been associated with a weakening of Commodity Prices. After two years of sustained increases, many non-oil commodity prices had began to decline in 1996 and 1997, mainly those of interest to Developing Countries. Increased Flexibility of the initiative of certain conditions of determining country eligibility, as well as promptness in implementation, are the real ground realities for ensuring a lasting and rapid solution to the "debt crisis" of not only Africa but also in other Regions.

The United States recovered by investment, which has brought about a significant increase in productivity, particularly in manufacturing goods. Japan could reap the benefits of its fiscal packages, growing at 3.5% in 1996 and of the same level during 1997 after a prolonged recession phase. This has been greatly owing to the depreciation of yen against the dollar. Now, the performance of the Japanese economy will mainly depend on reduction in budget deficit and increasing exports.

It is expected that if monetary policy is tightened in the United States of America, its affects may not be limited to widening the global deflationary gap. Alongwith this, if upward pressure on the dollar is kept, the effect might multiply, rather than to reduce, trade imbalances.

New Paradigms in International Economics

The big recent paradigm of the World Economy is the existence of unleasing of Market forces. The deregulation of domestic markets and their opening up to international competition have become universal features. The "invisible hand" of, Adam Smith, new operates globally and with fewer counter-failing pressures. Many International Economists are optimistic about the prospects for faster growth and for convergence of incomes and living standards which greater global competition will bring.

Presently with globalisation, capital, technology and enterprise have become mobile factors of production. Further, within the groups of countries formation of a labour block has also become a mobile agent Moreover, skilled and technical labour is more mobile than ordinary/unskilled labour among the different countries. Further, multinational companies are making the services of land more and more mobile. Thus, with free mobility of factors of production, International Economics theory is undergoing a tremendous change.

However, there is also another big paradigm in the International Economy i.e. widening income gaps. Since, the early 1980s the World Economy has been characterised by rising inequalities and slow growth. Income gaps between the North and South have further widened. In 1965, the average per capita income of the G 7 countries as was 20 times that of the World's poorest seven countries, now it is more than 39 times as much. No doubt, some of the developing countries are growing faster than Industrial countries, but nevertheless not fast enough too narrow the absolute per capita income gap.

Further, growing wage inequality between skilled and unskilled workers, gaining of capital in comparison with the labour, rapid expansion of Public and Private Debt, Agricultural price liberalisation have not boosted the income of farmers are such problems, which are going to become global day by day.

Most of the recent accounts of the flying geese paradigm paint a harmoninous picture in which East Asian development is presented almost in entirely cooperative terms, while the potentially conflictual and competitive aspects of this process are virtually ignored. The new trading regime under the WTO has reduced the scope for general forms of tariff protection, many trade related subsidies and performance standards and the tax enforcement of intellectual property rights. The Uruguay Round has clearly opened up new export opportunities for developing countries and improved their security of market acccess. Further, the agreement on Subsidies and countervailing measures defines "subsidies" for the first time, tightous the discipline on subsidies, and extends them to all W.T.O. member countries.

The WTO seems to have taken a cautious step towards correcting some of the anomalies in the multilateral trading system adversely affecting the interests of the developing countries. In its meeting held in May, 1998 at Geneva, acknoledged the fact that the three-year old WTO regime has not helped the poor countries in stepping up their exports. The same has also been confirmed by the studies conducted by the United Nations and other Institutions/ countries. More significantly, the liberalisation of trade in goods has proceeded very slowly in these sections of the International Economy where the developing countries, rightly emphasised the need for amendments in the Uruguay Round agreements in the services sector, agriculture and trade-related intellectual property rights. Now, a large proportion of liquidity growth stems from the Financial

Intermediation of Private Banking Institutions, as surplus funds flow-into the International Credit Markets and ultimately are lent onward to countries who are in deficits in balance of payments.

The largest part of the deficits has been financed by running-up foreign debts rather than by bringing down foreign reserves i.e. Liability Financing rather thank "Asset Financing" of imbalances.

The successful completion of the Uruguay Round in 1883 represented the most extensive multilateral trade agreement in the history of International Economics. Where after seven years of negotiations GATT's 117members reached at consensus on many contentious issues, including for the first time services, trade related investment measures, and intellectual property rights. The Round had barely drawn to a close, however, when consideration began about the agenda for future multilateral negatiations. This Round of negotiations was precedent for setting in linking trade policy, as a compliance mechanism, to non-trade objectives through the intellectual property decisions, and will continue as a competitive policy, with labour standards and trade and environmental improvements.

In the traditional approach, tariffs were to be reduced, but by and large, nations were left free to pursue domestic policies with regard to competition (anti-trust), environment, and labour standards. The deregulation of domestic markets and their spending up to International competition have become a universal paradigm. Hence, International Trade remained still a political act, whether it takes under a system of free trade or protection, of state trading or private enterprise, of most-favoured nation clause, or of discriminatory treatments.

The following aspects of the International Economy deserve special consideration:-

- To re-negotiate the debts of developing countries.
- To redefine the terms of trade and to assure greater access to Developed Market economies.
- To further improve the decision-making process of the IMF, IBRD and WTO.
- To attain the United Nations, Official Development Assistance targets.
- Indexation of the Primary Commodities' prices with those of Manufacturing goods.
- To consider to create a Common Fund to help to stabilise commodities Prices of such products.

The present international economic order was evolved over a period of four decades or so, since the termination of the Second World War. The present order, in essence, is radically different from the order that obtained during the earlier period.

The present international economic order has, without any doubt, brought about unprecedented prosperity and material welfare in the global polity. The unprecedented growth of technology, manufactures and agricultural product have been witnessed over the past few decades. However, unwittingly, the present order has also thrown in some challenges which need be faced boldly, and if necessary even by giving a new shape to the system.

First, of all the present order is characterised by the creation and widening of the gap between the rich and the poor states; the gap can be seen in the form of large differences in the per capita income of poor and rich nations—on an average the per capita income of poor countries is hardly 1/50 of that obtaining in an industrially advanced country. Not only this gap has come to subsist, and projections for future provide that the gap may indeed widen.

Secondly, the present system is not essentially based

on free enterprise and free markets, because it is guided and manipulated in these respects. In actual practice in place of open and expanding trade we see a tariff system with low tariffs for raw-materials and high tariff for industrial products. This has blocked the Industrialisation of the poor countries. The flow of capital and the credit system is also dominated by United States, European countries and the oil producing countries. There is no free flow of technology and the system of regulating the ownership of patents, which restricts the use of those patents to rich countries.

Finally, the notion of readily available raw materials is also virtually non-existent because we are confronted with the threat of scarcity.

Thus, we find that the present international economic system is not as free as it often claimed. The present system is largely guided and manipulated for the benefit of rich countries. If we are genuinely interested in finding a solution to the problem of an equitable division of property, of scarcity of natural resources and of depollution of the environment, the only solution lies in the New International Economic Order.

New International Economic Order

The Less Developed Countries (LDCs) have been making persistent demands for introducing fundamental reforms in the economic, commercial and financial relationships between themselves and the developed countries. The call for New International Economic Order is based on the assumption that the prevalent international order perpetuates and aggravates international inequalities and that new relationship of interdependence should replace the older patterns of dependence and unequal exchange. It is argued by the advocates of New International Economic Order that the rich developed countries and that it is in their self interest to encourage the promotion of growth and development of the poor countries in order to expand their markets.

The less developed countries hold the view that the Developed Countries must recognise the growing power of the commodity producers as evident from the success of Organisation of Petroleum Exporting Countries (OPEC) in raising oil prices, and accept that the locus of power has inclined in their favour.

The New International Economic Order embodies exhaustive and ambitious purpose. The main objective is no less than the creation of a new structure of economic relationships, warranting fundamental changes in a large number of related field—commodity trade, market access and preference, aid flows, the activities of multinational corporations, the international monetary system, the restructuring of international institutions, the transfer of technology, etc.

Goals and Means

New International Economic Order deals both with goals and means. The goals which are rather more evident from all the UN conferences held on this issue, lay emphasis on the desire for a more just distribution of world economic resources among the countries—rich as well as poor.

In the wake of the oil crisis in 1973, the OPEC countries with a little below 300 million people have been able to raise their incomes sharply. The rest of the poor countries with about five times people have rather been placed in more precarious position. The oil crisis helped only a handful of countries—some of whom were already rich—whereas the vast majority lost by it. The poor remain poor. The "25 poorest countries" are mentioned in world forums but no practical action has so far been initiated to help these nations. Besides the need of making NIEO's benefit available to the poorest states has not been given serious thought. The developed countries are putting up firm resistance against it. Another reason is that the less developed countries have already suffered so much at the hands of Super Powers that these states now stand inflexibly on the principle of sovereignty and do not allow any foreign country or the UN to interfere in their internal affairs.

Mini-Income Target: The New International Economic Order sets forth another goal to create a material minimal standard of living, a mini-income for those who are facing harsh economic realities. Its purpose is to persuade the rich countries to bring reforms in the international economy. As owing to various reasons, the principle of sovereignty will play a decisive role in relation to UN also in the near future, such a goal should practically imply that the rich countries accepted such reforms within NIEO which would be instrumental in creating a mini-income for the poorest countries and that their aid for development would be channelled to poorest countries and in particular to those countries which carry out a conscious policy of levelling and justice inside their own borders.

Parts and the Whole : There are three parts of entity embodying the NIEO. The first is to the extent to which the developing countries can force the rich countries to a more just distribution of world income than the one we have today. For instance, the price policy of the OPEC cartel, which in one stroke was able to redistribute about a couple of per cents of world income from the rich to the oil producing countries. Several raw material countries are dreaming about how by acting in the similar manner, they could form the cartels also for other raw materials and force the developed countries to pay many a times higher than that the importers pay now.

The second factor is that of morality that the rich

should share their wealth with less developed countries.

The third and most important motive behind the NIEO is of a materiality more concrete future. It emphasizes that it is in the common interest of developing and industrial countries alike to elaborate an NIEO; for example, both sides can have a common interest in a reduction in the fluctuation of prices of raw materials and therefore accept certain stabilization agreements; the governments in rich countries could come to find that it would be in the interest of the large consumer groups to import cheaper goods from the developing countries, although it could hit some home industries and its workers whose problems would have to be solved in another way—through labour market policies.

These three parts—*the threat, the morals,* and the *common interests,* can said to be the main parts in the entity called NIEO. However, the entity is greater than and different from the parts comprising it.

The Means or the Instrument of Economic Policy

The means for realising the NIEO are basically instruments of economic policies which can be mutually devised by the developed countries and less developed countries. The NIEO can be realised through international trade. The LDCs want better financial possibilities to develop their economies. They want to have a greater inflow of one of the most dynamic development factors—science and technology—and at the same time these countries opt for exercising control over its composition. The developing countries aspire for acquiring help as well as industrialisation and development in agricultural sector. Besides, these countries want a greater formal as well as real power in the decisive institutions which govern the international economic development, especially the entire UN system.

Foreign Trade: The major demands of the LDCs in respect of foreign trade are they want higher prices on their export goods, some sort of guarantee of a similar development for export and import prices and better possibilities for facilitating admission to the markets of the rich countries.

The case of export cartel of the OPEC countries, with a four fold doubling of the oil prices, has provided an impetus to the developing countries. It has motivated the raw materials exporting countries to search out the possibilities of creating other cartels for raw materials between the developing countries or if this does not work out, at least some sort of international raw material agreements which should provide the developed countries good prices and Ability in their countries.

There are possibilities that effective cartels might perhaps be formed in the bauxite or copper production on the model of oil cartels. But it is doubtful if cartel method would be successful. The case of oil export is different. Even prior to the oil crisis, the oil export from the oil producing countries was about 50 percent larger than the sum of the five next most important export commodities of the less developed countries—copper, coffee, sugar, cotton and natural rubber. Currently, the oil export from the developing countries is almost exceeding the sum of all other exports from them. Another factor disfavouring cartel system is that it redistributes the profits from trade in an unsystematic manner. This system helps only rich countries whereas the countries like India and Bangladesh are losers. Moreover, developing countries are not the only countries which export raw materials. The United States, the Soviet Union and a host of other developed countries are more benefited from cartel system than the developing countries.

There are proposals to create raw material agreements between the rich and developing countries. The past experience reflects the unsuccessful misled of such attempts. Both rich and poor countries share a common interest in a certain stability in price development and perhaps some practical results can be worked out in this direction. The expectations that such stabilisation agreements at the same time should envisage a price policy which severely redistributes gains from rich to poor countries, cannot be particularly high. The endeavours to relate import and export price development for the less developed countries with the help of indexing appear to be too complicated to yield quicker results.

Better recourse for the developing countries is to open their own markets in the developed countries for exporting their products. The developed countries can provide protection to the interest of less developed countries. Mutually agreed norms can be worked out with a view to distribute the burden justly.

Development Aid: It is widely argued that the rich countries should contribute one per cent of their total production to the developing countries. The poor countries should share the development expertise of the rich countries. Development aid is a powerful means to realise the objectives of NIEO quicker and sooner.

Another way through which developed countries can help the LDCs is the writing-off of old debts or putting a moratorium over it. The poor countries which are mostly indebted too, should in this way get an extra assistance, which would be valuable. This type of measure can easily be carried through politically in the rich countries than development and to the same tune.

Science and Technology: The developing countries require and in their scientific and technological development, technical assistance provides gains and savings which can further be invested in economic development. However, scientific and technological know-how is precisely not under the direct control of the states but under the control of multinational enterprises. These transnational corporations do not use science and technology in the interest of developing countries but more in their monopolistic interests. A study conducted by the UNCTAD reveals that of all patents in the world, about six percent are owned by the less developed countries. Other about 84 per cent is owned by the multinational corporations operating in the developing countries. And of these only 5 percent is used in production. The transnational enterprises are there to thwart the efforts of others from starting production of the goods patented that is a protection against competition. In reality, the patents of the multinational corporations effectively discourage all indigenous national efforts in the developing countries to develop their productivity with the help of modern technology.

The Soviet Union and Japan have made considerable development by copying and imitating foreign techniques. For realising the objectives of the NIEO, it is necessary that developing countries should scrap the present patent system and work out norms authorising the developing countries with rights to produce any technique which they are capable of producing. It has to be ensured that such a system of rules is not exploited by the Multinational Corporations.

Industry and Agriculture: Much has been said in the domain of industry and agriculture in the international forums. No new special proposals have come forward in regard to the NIEO. It is well known that developing countries want to raise their degree of industrialisation. The process of industrialisation can not be had in isolation. The process entails the involvement of industrialised countries. It is not clear how far these industrialised countries are willing to help and cooperate with the developing countries. The developing countries which share seven per cent of industrial production during the recent session of the General Assembly of the UN, wanted to establish a principle that they (developing countries) should be entitled to "a larger percentual share of world industrial production." This demand of developing countries was strongly opposed by the representatives of the European Community and Japan. Developed countries were willing to accept only that the developing countries are entitled to a "larger industrial production."

Agriculture is another realm where developed countries are reluctant to cooperate with the developing countries. The United States has the greatest export surplus which can be used for help in starvation or disaster. This can perhaps help in feeding the millions in the poorest countries. But inside the United States, there are lobbies which hold the view that food assistance to developing countries helps in augmenting population "uncontrollably," that America cannot alone finance the food deficit of the developing countries. A section in America is of view that the Soviet Union can purchase the whole surplus and that food can be used as a weapon like oil. However, the developed countries can afford to share their food surplus with the poor countries.

Share in Decision-making: *The New York Times*. In a leading article in May 1975 about how to save UNO, wrote, "The reason why the UN General Assembly does not funtion now is that countries with 10 per cent of world population and 5 percent of its production can marshal as two thirds majority inthe General Assemly. Half of this number can stop Soviet-American proposal and have done it. "The developing countires have thus great powerin the UN General Assembly. But in General Assembly no real decisions are taken. It adopts only resolutions and principles which cannot force others to act on it. However, the powerful bodies where decisions are taken and can be enforced are the Security Council of the UN, the World Bank and other important economic organisations. The developing countries have little or no power in these important world bodies. These are dominated by the developed countries. It is because of this reason that the resolutions inside the UN system often get a progressive and in relation to the problems of the developing countries very positive form whereas the positive actions continue not to be taken or to be minimal. The gap between words and action widens.

NIEO—The Basis

A new International Economic Order (NIEO) is the only alternative that can go a long way in securing an equitable partnership between the rich and the poor nations. The issue of securing NIEO can be legitimately described as the most vital issue of contemporary international relations. The first two decades after the Second World War were dominated by the decolonisation movement, and these witnessed the rise of a number of sovereign independent states in Asia and Africa. These new states, being motivated by a strong desire for development and full participation in international relations, started working for securing their due rights and roles in international relations. However, the abject poverty, scarcity of resources and under development that characterised their people made it difficult for them to secure the desired objectives. Their dependence upon the developed and rich countries, particularly for their economic needs, forced them to live with the domination of the international system by the rich and powerful states. The rich countries came up with several instruments like foreign aid, Multinational Corporations, IMF, SDR etc., which were apparently designed to help the poor countries but which were in reality the instruments for perpetuating their neo-colonialist control over their former colonies. The new states found themselves in a situation in which despite the sovereign independent statuses, they found themselves dependent upon the rich for meeting even their primary needs. Their dependence was exploited by the developed countries for influencing their economies and policies. The international economic system was and continues to be exploited by the rich states to their own advantage and the net result came in the form of a big gap between the rich and the poor. Inequalities and imbalances in international economy and trade that came to be developed as a result of the protectionist and neo-colonial policies of the developed nations, created a situation in which the poor underdeveloped countries found themselves being squeesed into being economic dependencies and satellites of the developed countries. The international economic system became more partial and exploitative. The energy crisis of 70s and several other harmful developments, made the underdeveloped countries totally dissatisfied with the prevailing system. They started making efforts towards the securing of their rights vis-à-vis the developed states. The existence of several international movements like NAM, Afro-Asian Solidarity Movement, Third World Unity and consolidation drive etc, provided them with the opportunity to share their problems and thoughts. The net result came in the form of the demand for restructuring of the international economic system—the creation of a new international economic order, with a view to make it equitable and just, and to end the existing system which was partial in favouring the interests of the developed countries, and which was giving little help to the third world countries towards the securing of their goals of development. The demand for NIEO has, however, failed to carry much conviction with the developed countries. They are in no mood to accept the demand as its acceptance is bound to end their existing superior position and role in international relations. Their opposition to the demand has come in the form of consolidation of their collective economic power as well as in the form of attempts to delay or evade the conduct of global negotiations over the issue. The commitment and determination of the Third World countries to secure NIEO versus the attempts of the developed countries to torpedo the demand have together made the issue of NIEO a burning issue of contemporary international relations.

Since early 1970s the issue of New International Economic Order has been the frontal issue in international relations involving the developing countries or the Third World on the one side and the developed countries or the first Two Worlds on the otherwise. The former regards the restructuring of the existing international economic order as the only way to get out of their present problems of poverty, scarcity, economic problems, imbalances and under—development. By this step alone can the existing era of neo-colonialism can be ended and Third World countries can become really free politically as well as economically. As against this, the developed countries appear in no mood of accepting a total change of existing economic order as it is bound to involve a decrease in their role in international relations and a burden on their economies. They advocate that the existing system, through several reforms and well planned and executed steps, alone can secure the desired changes in international economic system. They regard the existing economic institutions and instruments of international economy as the best available means for securing development of the Third World countries. They, therefore, oppose the demand for the total restructuring of international economic order—i.e. the demand for NIEO.

This difference of approach between the developed and under developing countries has made the issue NIEO as the most vital issue in the relations between them. Since early 1970's the debate on a NIEO has opened a new chapter in international relations. It can be legitimately described as one of the key issues of contemporary international relations.

Infact, the qualitative change in the nature of International Politics form a subject studying power and security in international relations to a subject studying the issues of "development," "welfare," "economic order among nations" has appeared because of the continuing debate on NIEO. Presently, socio-economic issues and the struggle and assertiveness by the underdeveloped countries form a vital core of international relations.

What is NIEO: NIEO constitutes a framework for eliminating the existing era of international economic system which, with all its features, is mostly catering to the needs and interests of the developed countries to the detriment of the underdeveloped, the Third World. It stands for making the international system fairer, just and equitable by adopting a code of conduct for the developed countries and by accepting the due rights of the underdeveloped countries. It is regarded as the only way to end the existing neo-colonial control that the developed countries are continuing to exercise over the newly emerged sovereign independent nations which constitute the Third World, it stands for arresting the widening gap between the "*spectacularly growing developed countries*" and the "*lagging behind developing countries.*" It seeks to end the existing imbalances and inequalities in the economic relations between the underdeveloped and the developed worlds. It seeks to end the existing monopolistic control of the developed countries over international trade, economy technological know—how and international economic institutions.

In simple words, New International Economic Order constitutes a frame—work for ending the existing anarchy in international economic system which is being utilised by a small number of developed countries for their own advantage and for maintaining their neo-colonial control over the underdeveloped countries. It stands for eliminating the exiting imbalances and inequalities by restructuring the existing international economic system and institutions. It seeks to secure an equitable and fairer distribution of world income and resources as can enable both the developed worlds and the Third World to develop side by side.

Need for NIEO: The emergence of a strong demand for a New International Economic Order has been largely due to the sharp and big changes in the international system of the post-war period. Initially,the weakened position of Europe, the rise of two super powers, the emergence of cold war, the rise of strong anti-imperialist and anti-colonialist movement, the emergence of a rapid process of decolonisation etc., were responsible for changing fast the political map of the world and the contents of relations among nations. Later on, the rise of new consciousness among the newly emerged countries of Asia, Africa and Latin America, the constitutions created by the détente between the two-superpowers, the example of economic recovery secured by European countries, the rise of local leviathans like India and Brazil, the change form confrontation to limited confrontation in the relations between USA and USSR and a host of other factors were responsible for bringing into focus the economic dimension of international relations. The commitment of the new states—the Third World, to secure socio-economic development and to play their due role in international relations further brought a big change in international relation.

In early 1970s, international relations came to be dominated by economic issues. Around this time a new kind of configuration emerged in international relations. It undermined the ideological overtones of the cold war era and brought into focus economic issues of development and underdevelopment. The conflict between Socialist East and Capitalist West came to be over stepped by the conflict between the excolonial underdeveloped poor 'have-nots' of the Southern Hemisphere. The Third World, on the one hand, and the economically developed and technologically advanced haves of the Northern Hemisphere—The two developed worlds. As a result, new economic consciousness and the conflict between the developed and the underdeveloped countries in international relations together found a manifestation in the form of North-South controversy over the issue of a new international economic order.

Factors that have Influenced the Demand for NIEO

The emergence of the demand for NIEO has been largely due to the following factors:

The Big North South Gap: A yawning economic gap exists between the developed and the lowly developed countries. The North with nearly 30% of world population controls more than 70% of world's income and wealth. The South has to satisfy the needs of more than 70% of world population with the help of less than 30% of resources. The per capita income of the two dozen industrialised countries is between $ 3000 to $ 6000, where as that of 125 developing countries is about $ 100. In the words of *Jan Tinberger*, "We have today about 2/3rd of mankind living on less than 30 cents a day. We have today a situation where there are about one billion illiterate people around the world. Although the world has both the means and technology to spread the education. We have nearly 70% of the children in the Third World suffering from malnutrition, although the world has the means to feed them. We have mal-distribution of worlds resources on the scale where the industrialised countries are consuming world's resources on a scale about 20 times more than the resources than the poor countries. We have a situation where in the Third World, millions of people toil under a burning sun from morning till dusk for miserable reward and premature death without discovering the reason why?" The wide gap between the North and the South seriously limits the scope of economic relations and trade between them. The affluence of the developed compared with the poverty, scarcity and underdevelopment that prevail in the lowly developed countries makes the international system imbalanced. While the outbreak of a big famine in Ethiopia and several other African states reflects the poverty of the South, the star was programmes and the continued arms race highlights the richness of the North. The South as such stands totally dissatisfied with the existing economic system.

Ever Widening Gap. The big economic and development gap that exists between the North and the South has been increasing at an alarming rate. The developed are becoming richer and the underdeveloped are becoming poorer, particularly after 1970s. By virtue of being technologically advanced and industrially developed, the countries of the North are strengthening their control over international trade and income. Both UNCTAD and GATT have virtually failed to prevent the widening gap between the rich and the poor. The record of UNCTAD clearly shows that the efforts of the developing countries to attain self-sustained growth have not received adequate support. The pattern of international trade continues to favour the developed countries. The energy crisis, the falling exports, the stiff competition in world market, the monopolistic role of the Multinational corporations, the inadequacy of Bretten Wood in the Contemporary times, the inadequate and limited foreign aid to the developing countries etc., have all combined to perpetuate and increase the gap between the North and the South.

"A combination of the persistent monetary crisis, exacerbated by inflationary trends and balanced of payment problems, continued deterioration in terms of trade and aid, prevalent draught conditions and above all the recent energy crisis have brought to the fore the array of grave economic social problems for the Third World. The stark realities of economic conditions in the Third World are too grim to be ignored." The gap between the per capita incomes of the rich nations and the poor nations is widening. For example, the share of the developing nations in world trade declined from 21.8% in 1960 to 17.6% in 1970. Though the report for 1984 appears encouraging yet the continuance of the trend towards a decline in the world trade share of the Third World continues to be there. The transfer of resources to the Third World is continuously declining while their external debt has been continuously increasing rather multiplying. The increase in the oil import bill of the developing countries has further hit hard their economies. This ever-widening gap has been a source of big dissatisfaction for the Third World countries and they regard NIEO as the only way out.

Increased Global Interdependence but Continued Low Role of the South: Despite the big gap that exists between the developed and the underdeveloped countries, the global interdependence has increased in our times. Both the developed and the under developed world today find themselves increasingly dependent upon each other. In the words of *Edward L. Morse*. "Evidence for the existence of a high level of interdependence in certain areas of the international system abounds. The recent global problem in respect of energy resources, the frequent currency crisis after 1967, and the suspicious raised of Soviet and American intentions in the Strategic Arms Limitation Talks bear testimony to the fact that international, and even predominantly domestic events have an increasingly deeper impact on a growing number of political systems throughout the world." The developed countries find themselves dependent upon the underdeveloped countries for the purchase of raw materials and for the sale of manufactured goods. The economic prosperity of the rich stands linked up with the purchasing power of the poor. The underdeveloped also continue to depend upon the developed countries mainly for: (i) securing economic, technological and industrial aid; (ii) selling their commodities;

and (iii) securing access to advanced technology.

However, due to the big and ever-increasing gap that exists between the North and the South, the global interdependence continues to be exploited by the former for strengthening their economic conditions. The hope that the developed countries would come forth with international actions augmenting the transfer of resources and liberalisation of trade, has proved to be wrong. In actual practice the developed countries have failed to appreciate properly, the importance of interdependence and have continued to pursue their desired objectives in the global international trade and economy without much regard to the perceptions and needs of the developing countries. Backed by three powerful weapons—technological, political and military power, the developed countries have maintained successfully their control and superior role in international economic order. This has been a source of grave dissatisfaction for the underdeveloped countries. 'The concept of interdependence existed the prospects of increased and active participation of the developing countries in international decision-making, however, much to their disappointment, they find themselves playing a secondary role in the ear of neocolonialism.'The underdeveloped countries now fully realise the partial nature of the existing economic system and hence advocate a new economic order.

Neo-colonial Control of the North over South: Despite the fact of global interdependence and the sovereign equal status of all the members of international community, the underdeveloped countries find themselves living in an era of neo-colonialism in which the developed countries continue to control their economics and policies. The dawn of independence and the resulting sovereign status has made them free only politically, economically and in actual practice they continue to be dependent upon the development countries. Being poor and under developed with abject poverty and scarcity of essential goods as their "assets," they find themselves helplessly dependent upon the developed for securing aid and help for meeting their primary needs and desires. They are very sore of the situation because they feel, and quite rightly so, that their present position is the result of the exploitation that they suffered during the past several centuries of their existence under the yoke of western imperialism. Their former colonial masters are the present day rich and developed nations. These could develop only because of their ability and success in exploiting the wealth and resources of their colonies. Even now they continue to exercise a neo-colonial control over the economies and policies of the developing countries. "The essence of neo-colonialism,' observes *N. Nkrumah,* "is that the state which is subject to it is, in theory, independent and has all the outward trapping of international sovereignty, in reality its economic system and thus its internal policy is directed from outside. "Though several subtle devices like foreign aid, military help, alliance, partnership, interventions, multinational corporations international economic policies etc., the developed countries are in a position to maintain and increase their control over existing international economic order and the economies and policies of the developing countries. The attempts of the developing countries to get rid of neo-colonialism have found manifestation in their demand for a new international economic order.

Excessive and One-sided Exploitation of World Income and Resources by the Developed Countries: Another fact of the relations between developed and underdeveloped countries is the continued disproportionately large exploitation of world resources and income by the former. Under multifarious disguises the stronger and rich countries are successful in maintaining the appropriation of world resources to the detriment of poor and weak countries. Being technologically and industrially advanced and economically affluent, the developed countries continue to have virtual control over the raw material markets, what partically amounts to a monopoly over manufactured products and capital equipment. They have been able to proceed at will in fixing the prices of the raw materials that they take from the developing countries. Consequently, they are in a position to drain the resources and income of the Third World, and put unhealthy pressure on the poor countries. For example on 8th May 1990, the IMF at its meeting adopted a US sponsored proposal which sought to link the 50% increase in its quota with the provision for the suspension of a member of failure to repay its arrears. It was a device to get legalised pressure tactics. That is why it was described by the Indian Foreign Minister as unfair and draconian.

The control of international economic institutions and world economy further strengthen the hold of the developed over the developing countries. By virtue of their dominant position the developed minority finds it easy and expedient to determine at will the allocation of world resources in tune with their desired objectives. "The will to gain and cling to their position of dominance over world resources has been the guiding principle of the behaviour of the developed countries." This has been a source of much disappointment for the developing countries. They want to end this domination of the developed countries by securing a fairer and just new international economic order.

The Inglorious and Hegemonic Role of the Multinational Corporations: Through a large and extensive between of transnational/multinational corporations, the developed countries have been exercising an unhealthy and undesirable control over the economics and policies of the developing countries. MNCs are owned by the developed countries and these function as their extra-governmental arms for extending their control over markets, economies and policies of the developing countries. A large number of industries in the developing countries are owned by these MNCs. Many international patents are controlled by them. They have a monopolistic control over advanced technology. There are about 5000 gaint MNCs of seven countries U.S.A., U.K., France, FRG, Italy, Japan and Canada which are controlling more than 50% of the world production. These corporations virtually control the natural resources and raw materials that are found in abundance in the under-developed countries. By virtue of their monopolistic position, the MNCs make huge profits through their industries and centres in the developing countries. Even a country like India, which is definitely more developed than other developing countries, continues to suffered economic exploitation at the hands of several MNCs.

The MNCs have created and are still creating several barriers aimed at checking the "access to markets" and "access to advanced technology" efforts of the developing countries. These corporations have the ability to check the rate of economic growth and development and to mould the way of industrial and economic development in the under-developed countries in a way as is deemed ideal to the interests of the MNCs. The barriers to entry created by the MNCs can hardly be countered by the developing countries through any negotiations. Here the developing countries are most vulnerable. "Their exports, be it of manufactured commodities or of primary products, are under the dominant influence of the operation of Trans-national Corporations. Nearly 40% of the world trade is intra-firm trade. The developing countries often find it very difficult to get their due share in world trade because of the monopolistic role of the MNCs." The MNCs have a formidable control over the international trade and these have effected deep peneterations into the economies of the developing countries. The developing countries are sick of the situation and they advocate an end to MNC menace in international economic trade and industrial relations.

For this purpose they demand a new international economic order.

The Failure of the Bretten "Voods: The underdeveloped countries have now fully realised the inherent-weaknesses and absolute partial and harmful nature and working of the existing international economic systems. The recurrent monetary crisis which have come to characterise the prevailing international economic system, the failure GATT and UNCTAD, the difficulties in the way of securing and using "Special Drawing Rights," the teaming large payments deficits and increased external indebtedness of the under-developed countries, reflects fully the failure of the Bretten Woods and the existing international trade system. In fact, in almost every way existing international system is proving to be a big failure for the countries of the Third World. It is in no meaningful way helping these countries to secure the desired goal of "development." The Third World, therefore, demands a restructuring of international economic system in such a way as shall ensure fair and just distribution of world income, resources and trade among all the countries. This demand has got christianied as the issue of New International Economic Order, and it stands for a new economic system capable of securing the development economic, technological and industrial, or the under-developed side by side with the developed.

All these factors have combined to make the Third World countries rally around the demand for NIEO as they consider it as the way to end their neo-colonial existence in the contemporary era of international relations.

Major Issues of New International Economic Order

The concept of the New International Economic Order involves several themes and issue which the underdeveloped countries desire to settle through global negotiations, more particularly through a North—South dialogue. The following are the major theme of the concept of NIEO:

Restructuring of World Economic Relations. The first theme of NIEO is the urgent need for restructuring the world economic relations on a just and reasonable basis. The existing economic relations are characterised by the developing countries as "anachronistic and irrelevant". Realising the non-viable nature of the existing economic order, the developing countries advocate a new economic order based on equality, interdependence mutual benefit and support for the rights of all nations to work for securing progress, development and a chance for a fair share in world wealth and income.

Institutional Changes. In the jargon of contemporary international relations, two institutional changes are deemed essential for safeguarding the rights and securing the needs of the under-developed vis-à-vis the developed countries. First relates to the restructuring of the existing rules and regulations governing the international economic relations, and second relates to the formation of new institutions and systems of cooperation among nations. Presently, the rules governing international economic and trade retains as well as the international institutions responsible for realising an enforcing these rules and regulations are such, as favour the interests and needs of the developed countries. The World Bank, the IMF, the conventions governing "Intellectual property" (patents, copyright etc.) and other economic institutions stand dominated by the developed countries. GATT is more conducive to the interests of the rich and developed countries. As such NIEO seeks to restructure these rules and institutions wit a view to make these useful for all without any bias or discrimination.

End of Protectionism in International Economy and Trade. The concept of NIEO stands for eliminating the existing system of protectionist trade and policies which is destined by the developed countries to safeguard their interests in international economy and trade. By several protectionist trade and economic policies the developed countries are in a position to impose discriminatory limits on exports to other countries and to make the world trade highly competitive—to the direct and big disadvantage for the developing countries. Discriminatory limits on exports and imports, even against the GATT rules, are frequently made and pressed into use by the developed countries. The past record of international trade bears testimony to this charge. Australia, Canada, France, the United Kingdom, the United States and Sweden have imposed new quotas and so called 'orderly marketing arrangement on the developing countries exports of footwear. A new protocol of the Multi-Fibre Arrangement, covering the period through 1981, the permitted imposition of more severe restrictions on clothing and textile. Under it, the ECM reduced 1978 quotas for three countries beneath the actual 1976 levels and severely limited the growth of quotas of other countries, including many that are only beginning to export these exports. Analysing the bad effects of such protectionist policies and trade, on the economies and international trade of the developing countries. A President of the World Bank. Mr. McNamara in one of his speeches observed. "The net effect of all these restrictive measures will be to limit the growth of developing countries' export of clothing and textile on only 5% per annum over the next few years compared to some 16% per annum in the period of 1967-76. The European Community and United States have introduced special protective measures regarding steel, which pose serious difficulties for those developing countries now emerging as exporters. UK has imposed quotas on television sets from the developing countries and similar action has been threatened in the United States and elsewhere." Such protectionist trade and policies have been a source of a big strain and loss for the developing countries. Their import bills have boomed while their exports have tended to be stagnant. The need is to end protectionism in trade and economy, and this is a vital theme of NIEO.

Transfer of Capital Resources. Another theme of NIEO is the actual transfer of capital resources alongwith the knowledge to put them to beneficial use in order to enable the underdeveloped countries not only to produce more for themselves but also to produce more for export to other countries. These transfers can take place either through private investment or economic aid channelled through official agencies both bilateral and multilateral. Cancellation of outstanding debts of the Third World countries and the grant of 0.7% of G.N.P. international as developmental aid to the developing countries can solve the capital needs of the entire Third World.

Transfer of Technology. Technology plays a key role in economic development. The inability of the developing countries to register a higher economic growth rate and development is largely due to the low-level of technology that is at their disposal. The recourse to advanced technology is vitally necessary for increased and efficient productivity. Its contribution, along with other factor's of production, is always substantial for all round development. For securing advanced technology the developing countries find themselves dependent upon the developed countries. The latter, through international patents and protective policies and measures have a virtual monopoly over advanced technological know-how and expertise. They are not prepared to transfer it to the developing countries without getting favourable commitments and several desired trade and economic agreements. Often their terms are not reasonable from the developing countries' point of view. Through NIEO, the Third World wants to systematise and facilitate the transfer of advanced technology from the developed to the developing countries.

Control over the Growing Menace of Multinational Corporations.

Presently, several multinational corporations (MNCs) are playing a big role in the spheres of international economy, trade technology and industrial production. They are controlling almost all the international patents in respect of advanced technological know-how. These are the instruments of the developed countries for maintaining their control over international economy and trade as well as for directing and controlling the economies and policies of the third World countries the developing countries are often forced by the developed countries to import the required technology through the expansion of cooperation with the MNCs which are held to be the most important channel for the transfer of capital technology and managerial expertise. However, this exercise involves high costs and heavy burdens for the developing countries. MNCs charge very high fees for the supply of advanced technology. With poor economic resources and poverty writ large, the developing countries find it very difficult, to purchase the technology from the MNCs. The fear of MNCs' interference with their domestic markets, economies, social and cultural values and decision-making further prevents them to deal with MNCs. The role of MNCs in international economy has been negative and damaging as it has been a source of maintaining and increasing the gap between developed and developing countries. These have always acted as instruments of neo-colonialism of the rich over the poor countries. These have often played a dirty role in securing the overthrow of elected governments in many developing countries. Dr. B.N. Mehrish, in his article; "India and the NIEO', has well summarised the Menace of MNCs in international relations: "The strategies of MNCs and their responses to governmental and international policies are such that of instead of increase in their share of benefit, the host countries lose some of the benefits stemming from the activities of multinational corporations. "Multinational Corporations are known to have applied diplomatic pressure to secure more favourable terms. They are a symbol of the 'international oligopoly." They have been trying to sabotage the development strategy formulated by the United Nations and refuse to meet the needs of the developing countries." Indeed, the role of MNCs in international economic and political relations has been unhealthy and harmful. The developing countries want an end to the menace of MNCs and for this advocate the formulations of a code of conduct for these corporations as a part of a new international economic order. "An essential ingredient in the new international economic order is, "writes Paul A. Tharp, "a set of policies to curb the monopolistic practices of the multinational corporations, especially in trade."

Recognition and Protection of the Interest of the Commodity Producers. In this era of global interdependence, the commodity producers—mostly the developing countries, are playing almost as important a role as is being played by the industrialised and advanced countries. However, the existing international economic order gives only marginal importance to the commodity producers. The lack of rules for safeguarding their interests make the developing countries live at the mercy of the developed countries. The dependence of the developing countries for the export of their commodities, the cut-throat unchecked open competition in international markets and protectionism in trade policies of the developed countries, together combine to make the lot of the Third World very poor and unfruitful. The developing countries want an international code of rules for protecting their trade interests. International agreements to raise and stabilise the prices of raw material products exported by developing countries have been a prominent theme in the new economic order. "The success of the producer cartels in oil and bauxite has stimulated interest in similar programmes for copper, tin, nickel, and primary products (Jute etc.) in general."

A Greater and Fixed Share in International Exports and a Total Revision of the Brettonwoods System. Another important theme of the New Economic Order is the securing of improved access to export markets in rich countries. The existing system unduly favours the rich *vis-a-is* the poor. In the presence of big economic and industrial gap between the developed and the developing countries. GATT and UNCTAD and failed to produce the desired effect and change in internal economic and trade system. Unregulated and open competition between the developed and the underdeveloped countries has proved to be a highly damaging aspect of international trade relations as it has always favoured the developed to the disadvantage of the underdeveloped. The Third World countries demands a definite fixed share in all international exports and tariff preferences in their favour as part of a new economic order. They argue that greater export sales facilitated by tariff preferences for developing countries and an end to shameful non-tariff barriers in some more developed countries would have a number of beneficial effects. With greater foreign exchange earnings, the developing countries could import the larger volume of capital goods and raw materials necessary to sustain more rapid growth of output, income and employment and thereby move towards development. The need is to end the existing terms of international economic relations and trade which are unfavourable to the Third World countries. GATT and UNCTAD have virtually outlived their existence and so is the case of the entire Brettonwoods System. Bretton woods has failed to create new truly global economic institutions for coordinating international economic relations. It has tended to favour the rich to the disadvantage of the poor. GATT has not been fully successful to secure greater trade liberalisation. Open competition among the developed and the developing countries has proved to be a barrier to the growth of the Third World. IMF has nearly failed to meet the developmental loan requirements of the third world. International economic institutions have come to be dominated by the rich and advanced countries. The Brenttewoods has failed to be adequately responsive to the needs of the developing countries. The need, therefore, is to replace it by a new economic system. The Third World demands a new system with a new set of priorities, principles procedures, and definite rules for governing contemporary international economic relations. The whole exercise should ensure the fulfilment of developmental needs of the developing countries as a part of total restructuring of international economic order on principles of equitable and just distribution of world income, resources and wealth among all the nations.

Self-Reliance. Finally, a major theme of NIEO is self-reliance. The developing countries aspire to move from underdevelopment to development. They want to be self-reliant—capable of satisfying the needs of their populations. This alone can ensure their effective and equal participations in international relations. The developing countries are fully aware that this objective can be achieved only by their own determination and efforts. However, they are also conscious of their present dependence upon the developed. For overcoming it, they want a new international economic order with a view to eliminate the existing partial and rich dominated international economic systems.

Mini-Income Targets. The NIEO involves a demand for creating a material minimal standard of living, a mini income for those who are facing harsh economic realities. The developed and rich countries should accept and introduced such reforms in the international system as can lead to fixed mini incomes for the poor and developing countries. This can go a long way to help the poor countries in their struggles to withstand he current economic hardships. Henry Kissinger, a former US Secretary of State, has rightly remarked that "International cooperation must be directed to the problems of creating a secure basic economic security for all and this challenge is above ideologies and block politics. No international order can be considered must if cooperation with the aim to raise the poorest of the world to a decent standard of living is one of its basic principles."

Conclusion. All these themes and issues together constitute the warp and woof of the concept of New international Economic Order. The developing countries are demanding: (i) a restructuring of the existing economic order; (ii) total recasting of the Brettenwoods System; (iii) an increased and definite share in world trade; (iv) writing off the old debts; (v) grant of international developmental aid; (vi) transfer of advanced technology by the developed countries; (vii) increased help for the development of agriculture and industry; and (viii) a due share in international decision-making. For achieving this, the Third World countries want a comprehensive North-South dialogue. They are also trying to develop through the promotion of South-South Cooperation for mutual development. The July 1985 conference of the ministers of the 'Group of 77' countries agreed to work out a mutual General Scheme for Tariff Preferences (GSTP) for the Third World countries. This is expected to facilitate and increase import—export relations among the developing countries. The luck-warm and almost evasive attitude of the developed countries has forced the Third World to go in for South-South Cooperation. The issue of NIEO has come to be a big controversial issue, rather the biggest issue in the relations between the two Developed Worlds and the Third World.

Emergence and Struggle of the Concept of NIEO

The evolution of the concept of New International Economic Order can be traced from mid-70s, more particularly from 1 May, 1974, because on this day, the sixth special session of the UN General Assembly adopted a "Declaration on the establishment of New International Economic Order" and thereafter several steps were initiated towards its achievement. Before 1974, NIEO was almost a theoretical and rhetorical phrase, after this Declaration it came to be practical action. The declaration proposed to replace the existing inequitable economic system as based upon the Bretton Woods proposals by a new intrnational economic sysem based upon the concept of equitable distribution of world income and resources. The new system was "to correct inequalities and redress existing injustices and ensure steady and speedy economic devlopment, peace and justice for present and future generations," and "to restore social justice in the world which has disappeared over decades of capitalism, imperisalism and the monopoly of technical talent."

The adoption of this declaration by the UNO was the result of consistent and persistent efforts of the Third World. The Afro-Asian Conference in Bendung (1955). Non-aligned conferences in Belgrade (1961) Cairo (1964), Lusaka (1970) and Algeria (1973) played an important role in strengthening international public opinion in favour of NIEO. In 1974, the UN General Assembly took up the discussion of raw material and development as it was recommended by the Algiers non-alignment summit. The sixth special session of UN General Assembly (9 April to 2 May, 1974) adopted the declaration for the establishment of NIEO. By this time, the western attitude underwent a change. Moving away from scepticism and indifference toword cooperation, governments began to show a growing readiness to seek the road to political stability and economic prosperity in a more rational way through negotiations. The raw material producing countries has also come of age. Politically, they were able to defend their sovereign rights, economically they seemed equipped to purse their national aspirations and internationally they appeared to be committed to seek cooperation.

The Principles adopted by the U.N. Sixth Special Session. The Declaration adopted by the Sixth special Session of the UN Assembly included the principles mentioned below:

(i) Full permanent sovereignty of every state over its natural resources and all economic activities including the right to nationalise or transfer its ownership to its nationals.

(ii) Right of all states and people to restitution and full compensation for the exploration and depletion of and damages to the natural resources and all other resource under foreign occupation or alien or colonial domination or apartheid.

(iii) Regulation and supervision of the activities of transnational corporations.

(iv) Just and equitable relationship between the prices of raw materials, primary products, manufactured and semi-manufactured goods exported by developed countries.

(v) Development aid without strings and flow of real resources to developing countries.

(vi) Transfer of science and technology to developing countries and improvement of their indigenous technology.

(vii) The need for all states to put an end to the waste of natural resources.

(viii) Facilitating the role of producer's associations in the sustained growth of economy and accelerating the development of developing countries.

Guidelines for Securing the above Principles. The resolution on NIEO laid down several guidelines with respect to the securing of these principles:

(i) Fundamental problems of raw materials and prime commodities related to trade and development.

(ii) International monetary system.

(iii) Industrialisation.

(iv) Transfer of technology.

(v) Regulation and control over the activities of transnational corporations.

(vi) Charter of Economic Rights and Duties.

(vii) Assistance in the exercise of permanent sovereignty of states over natural resources.

(viii) Strengthening the role of the UN system in the field of international economic cooperation.

Seventh Special Session of U.N. General Assembly. The General Assembly Seventh Special Session on Development and International Economic Co-operation in September 1975 served as a turning point in the North-South dialogue because of the realism displayed by both the Third World and the West in their negotiations. Sympathetic cooperation between the "group of 77' and the West resulted in a compromise resolution which, when implemented, will prove to be a long a awaited milestone in the path of the Third World's progress.

The Provisions of the 1975 Resolution. The basic provisions of the resolution read:

(i) The expansion and diversification of trade, improvement of productivity, and the increase of export earnings of the developing countries.

(ii) The attainment of stable, remunerative and equitable prices for exported raw materials.

(iii) The reduction or removal of tariff and non-tariff

barriers affecting the exports of the developing countries.

(iv) An increase in the volume and improvement of their term of development assistance.

(v) The attainment of the official development assistance target of 0.7 percent GNP of all donor countries by the end of this decade.

(vi) An increase in the developing countries access on favourable terms to world capital market.

(vii) The relief of debt burdens of the most seriously affected countries

(viii) Increasing international contact and surveillence over the creation and equitable distribution of world liquidity.

(ix) Facilitating the process of industrialisation in the developing world.

Lima Conference 1975. At the Lima conference of the Foreign Ministers of the Non-aligned nations, a convention establishing solidarity fund for economic and social development was approved. This fund was to be financed principally through voluntary contributions, and Kuwait offered to make an initial contribution of one billion dollars. It was further decided at this conference to establish a special fund financing buffer stocks of raw materials and primary products exported by the developing countries.

Parts Dialogue 1975. For analysing and improving the relations between the developed and developing nations, a conference was held in Paris in December 1975. Twenty-eight developing and developed nations attended this conference and discussed issue of international economic cooperations, and to initiate an intensified dialogue. The participates agreed to establish an international secretariat and 4 commissions: (i) Energy: (ii) Raw Materials; (iii) Development; and (iv) Financial Affairs. The developing countries were successful in persuading the developed countries to accept that there was a firm link between the problem of energy and the problem of development. However, nothing concrete could emerge on the issue of NIEO.

Colombo Summit of the Non-aligned. At the Colombo summit of the nonaliged nations (1976) it was agreed. (1) to mutually assist each other to reach an annual target of 4% in food and agricultural production in the next 10 years, (2) to initiate a plan of mutual cooperation to diminish their dependence on multi-national pharmaceutical companies, (3) to create a "Third World Bank's, (4) to explore ways and means of breaking communication barriers that separate these countries, and (5) to set-up a news agency pool to diminish their dependence on Western news agencies.

UN General Assembly Special Session 1980. Acting on the demand made by the Third World countries, the U.N. General Assembly met on 25 August 1980 in a special session for discussion the economic relations between the two developed worlds and the Third World. In this session, he Third World countries demanded increased aid, cancellation of their more than $360 billion debts, more free trade and guaranteed prices for raw-material. However, their demands produced little impact on the developed countries and consequently, the session failed to produce and tangible result except that it initiated the process for opening nine months of global negotiations, beginning from January 1981, which were designed to secure more frutful and equitable trade and economic relations between the developed and the developing countries. However, these negotiations also failed to make any real headway.

Cancun Summit 1981. Leaders of 14 developing and 8 industrialised Nations met in Cancun, Mexico, on October 22-23, 1981, to discuss the progress of North-South negotiation in the United Nations and other forums, It was described as an International Meeting on Cooperation and development.

Invitations were sent out to 23 nations of whom only the Soviet Union failed to respond. The Soviet Union described it as a "dialogue of the deaf" which could serve only to exemplify the differences between the developing and industrialized nations. Cuba, despite being the current chairman of the NAM, was not invited to the summit, since it was felt by the 11 co-sponsors that Cuban participation would precipitate the withdrawal of the United States.

The Cancun summit began on October 21, with President Lopez Portillo and Mr. Pierre Trudeau as co-chairmen. In his speech, President Lopez Portillo observed that international financial and trade institutions such as the IMF, the World Bank and the GATT had "depend resentment and frustration", since they tended to come" mere sounding boards" for the countries which dominated the voting.

U.S. President Reagan, while addressing the summit on the first day confirmed that the United States was prepared to take part in the global negotiations provided that the following conditions were met: (i) that global negotiations should be oriented towards specific areas; (ii) that they should not seek to create new international institutions, but should recognise the "competence, functions and powers" of existing international agencies; (iii) that they should be aimed at achieving greater international economic growth; and (iv) that they should be held in a cooperative atmosphere "rather than one in which views became polarised and chances for agreement are needlessly sacrified." Among other representatives of industrialised countries, President Mittrrand, Mr. Trudeau and Mr. Falldin all expressed support for the launching of global negotiations at the United Nations.

At the end of the meeting, Britain the U.S.A. and West

Germany maintained their view that negotiations on restructuring the world economy should take place in the relevant international agencies, while the other 19 leaders favoured placing ultimate authority over global negotiations in the United Nations. According to the summary of the proceedings issued by the two co-chairman (no official communique was issued). The heads of the state and government confirmed "a consensus to launch global negotiations on a basis to be mutually agreed in circumstances offering the prospect of meaningful progress." However, no agreed target date for their commencement was specified. This summit virtually failed to arrive at an agreed decision regarding future course of North-Southeconomic relations.

December 1981 Resolution and its Failure. In early December 1981, the representatives of the developing countries at the United Nations, drafted a resolution for the General Assembly proposing North-South negotiations on restructuring the international economy. However, because of the U.S. objections on the plea that it posed a threat to the independence of established economic institutions like World Bank and the IMF, the resolution was not taken up for discussion. Since the failure of this resolution no major resolution move have been made for securing North-South dialogue over NIEO.

South-South meet at New Delhi, 1982. With a view to secure increased economic and trade cooperation among the developing countries, as well as for securing coordination in their policies over the issue of the approach to be pursued within the Group of 77 (Now nearly 120 developing countries). India took the initiative to hold a meeting of the developing countires in New Delhi. The meeting took place on February 22-24, 1982 and was attended by the representatives of 44 developing countries. Mrs. Indira Gandhi in her opening speech expressed concern over what she described as "visible deterioration in the global economy since the Cancum summit", and she was especially critical of "protectionism in industrialised countries" which she said had "victimized the developing world". "Developing countries should close their ranks to withstand pressure from affluent nations."

The South-South cooperation conference agreed to concentrate upon the following points for further considerations. (i) The formulation of programmes for agricultural self-reliance and food self-sufficiency: (ii) the creation of a world bank "energy affiliate"; and (iii) the creation of a multi-lateral financing facility for joint ventures and technical cooperation among developing countries. On the last subject, an expert group was to be convened under Indian chairmanship to report back to the Group of 77.

The conference concluded with unanimous acceptance of the importance of cooperation for collective self-reliance, and with a renewed call for efforts to reach an agreement on the launching of North-South global economic negotiations.

South-South Cooperation GSTP July 1985. The idea of Global System of Trade Preference (GSTP) was mooted first in 1982 and took shape at the two UNCTAD meetings in 1984 which did the spadework. This idea was mooted for securing increased trade cooperation and relations among the developing countries.

The two day ministerial level meeting of the developing countries was held on 25-26, 1985 to consider GSTP as means for promoting South-South cooperation. The then Union Commerce Minister of India, Mr. V.P. Singh presided over the meeting which was inaugurated by Prime Minister Rajiv Gandhi. In his speech, the Prime Minister called upon the developing countries to work or collective self-reliance through boosting their trade. More than 70 countries which deliberated for two day on way of making South-

South cooperation meaningful and mature agreed that the negotiating committed (for GSTP) should consider across the board tariff reduction of upto ten percent in addition to a product-by-product approach. The GSTP declaration also unidentified sectors for particular social-economic importance for the developing countries such as processed tropical products, non-textile handicrafts, textiles and agricultural products for comprehensive and integrated treatment relating to tariff and non-tariff measures. Another important decision of meeting was to take up periodic reviews at political levels for monitoring and evaluation of the progress relating to GSTP, and that the next such meeting will be help in Brazil.

The Delhi meeting made a decisive breakthrough by approving to have a workable counterpart to the rich nations concept of the Global Scheme of Preferences. According to the time-table chalked out at the meeting, agreement incorporating ground rules were to be completed by October 31, 1985. The techniques and modalities were to be worked out by December 31, 1985, and a negotiating plan was to be drawn up by February 28, 1986. The first round of talks (negotiations) was to begin not later than May 1, 1986. This time-bound schedule was made to secure definite progress towards GSTP among the developing countries. In actual practice, however, no results were achieved. Talks were held but no agreement was made.

With title hope for an early North-South dialogue/ agreement over NIEO, the promotion at South-South cooperation constitutes the best way for the developing countries to develop. South-South cooperation constitutes a good step towards a defacto NIEO. NAM, Group of 77 and the Third World countries in all conferences have been trying hard to secure a North-South dilogue on NIEO, but their efforts have not yet been successful. As an alternative, a programme for South-South cooperation is gradually emerging. The Third World countries regard it as their best. NAM has taken a lead in this direction. The Eighth NAM summit decided to hold a full fledged conference of the nonaligned Foreign Ministers on South-South cooperation.

June 1987 Non-aligned Foreign Ministers Conference on South-south Cooperation. The pyongyang Conference, The first conference of Non-aligned Foreign Ministers on South-South cooperation was held on 12 and 13 June, 1987 at Pyonyang. It gave a call to give new impetus to cooperation among the non-aligned and other developing countries and adopt a new approach to make such cooperation among the non-aligned and other developing countries and adopt a new approach to make such cooperation more dynamic. The ministers while adopting the Pyongyang declaration, listed a number of measures to develop and strengthen economic independence of these countries which would build collective self-reliance and increase their bargaining power in negotiations with the North.

Reaffirming the unwavering commitment of all non-aligned countries to economic cooperation among themselves, the declaration noted that the current world economic crisis and the economic policy of some rich nations had a negative impact on the economies of countries of the south.

Referring to the indebtedness of developing countries, the declaration called for a political dialogue between the developed and the Third World Countries to resolve the problem uppaid debts.

Reiterating its demand for an international conference on money and finance for development at the earliest, the declaration expressed concern at the continuous decline incommodity prices and regretted that certain developed countries did not show the required political will to remove trade imbalance at the last Uruguay meeting.

An action plan, incorporated in the declaration, called for measures for economic cooperation at the national, regional and international levels to promote South-South cooperation.

The plan said competent professonal consultancy organisations available in developing countries must be tapped in a better way to implement various action oriented programmes.

It called for payments and clearing house arrangements to support expansion of trade among developing countries under the global system of trade preferences.

The adoption of the Pyongyang declaration and the plan of action adopted by this conference of 101 delegations from NAM countries could go a long way towards increasing and expanding cooperation among the developing countries in carrying forward the struggle for the NIEO. The Pyongyang Declarations gave a call for a political North South dialogue on the debt crisis—though a reiteration of earlier such appeals from other forums- came not a minute too soon. The Third World countries among themselves carry a debt burden of well over a trillion dollars and its repayment is running into great difficulties. Some African countries have to set apart as much as 40 to 60 percent of their annual export earning for debt servicing. Such indeed is the seriousness of the debt crisis that the rate of IMF loan disbursements has not fallen to less than the money it gets back from the debtor nations and the much flaunted Banker Plant has also failed to defuse the debt bomb. Unless urgent political talks are held between the North and the South to resolve this crisis, it could lead to a major economic disaster.

Commenting upon the Pyongyang Declaration, The Tribune in one of its editorials rightly observed, "The declaration has rightly stressed the inter-relationship between peace, disarmament and development because much of the Third World debt burden has been caused by avoidable purchase of weaponary from the developed countries. The high rate of obsolescence of sophisticated weaponry makes it imperative for them to go on allocating higher amounts for weapons purchases just to maintain what could be called the balance of terror in the world. A global disarmament arrangement is, thus, a necessary concomitant of a new international economic order. To the extent the deliberations at Pyonyang helped to expand mutual cooperation among the Third World countries and encourage South-South trade and economic cooperation to reduce their dependence on the rich countries by building up a regime of collective self-reliance, they will be planning a major role in saving the world from the gravest economic disaster it has faced since 1929."

Meetings of South-South Commission. The second meeting of South-South Commission for betterment of Third World countries was held at Kual Lumpur March 1988. In it the Malayasian PM Mr. Mahathir Mohammed urged the member states to formulate a multipronged strategy to combat the economic problems in developing countries brought on by statement in the implementation of the NIEO. The meeting, the first of its kind, dedicated itself to focus on issues of South-South co-operation for self-reliance and South-North relations. The commission which was presided over by former Tanzanian President Julius Nyerere was entrusted with the task of analysing and commenting on the evolving global environment as was being influenced by recent political, economic and technological changes in the North.

Till Today (1990) the South Commission has held, in all, seven sessions but its meetings have resulted into no concrete results.

The continued Neo-colonial control of the North over the economies and policies of the South, the protectionist policies adopted by the industrialised countries against the import of processed and unprocessed commodities from the Third World countries, the steep fall in their population, growth rate and the resultant slow-down in the growth of the inelastic demand for essential commodities, the persistent fall in the commodity prices over the past few years and the steady development of a rapid global movement toward an "international service and information economy" the changes in Eastern Europe containing the possibility of diversion of Foreign Aid from developed to the Eastern European states, have all made an imperative to usher in an era of South-South Cooperation for the sheer survival of the Third World countries." North is not agreeing in favour of NIEO. The South has only one alternative development through South-South cooperation.

Meeting of G-15. With a view to encourage and lead the drive for South-South cooperation, a three day summit meeting of the groups of 15 (G-15) Third World countries were held at Kuala Lumpur on 1 June 1990. It was designed to act as an 'Action Group' for the South. The leaders of G-15 made it clear that the Action Group was to be an elitist group of a rival competitor to South-South Cooperation; Group of 77 and NAM movements. They described its role as a catalyst group intended to invigorate action towards increased and mature South-South cooperation.

The joint communiqué issued after the G-15 meeting listed several agreements among the 15 developing countries for increasing South-South cooperation and for adopting an agreed stand at the Uruguay Round of trade talk under GATT. The communiqué declared "We affirm our commitment to a balanced and successful conclusion of the Uruguay Round of Multilateral Trade Negotiations which takes into account the concerns and needs of the developing countries. We shall closely consult each other and coordinate our efforts towards this end." "It gave a cal for increased

South–South cooperation, North-South cooperation, end of buyers conference, and immediate steps for securing GSTP among Third World countries," GSTP (Global System of Trade Preferences) among the Third World countries was accepted as a necessary and valuable vehicle for promoting trade and closer economic cooperation among them. It gave a call that the second round of negotiations be launched under GSTP as soon as possible.

Among other things, the group agreed on about a dozen projects for South—South cooperation, with three of them ready to be started off immediately. The other projects requiring more details would be worked on further, with the countries proposing them being responsible for the follow-up actions.

The co-operation projects include a trade financing facility, to start on a bilateral basis first among any two countries through guarantees of the respective central banks, while exports would meet and consult further on how this type of payment arrangements and guarantees could be multilateralised. The other two projects are the establishment of a South Investment. Trade and Technology data Exchange Centre, and of a Business and Investment Forum for the South.

The G-15 communique also covered a number of critical issues (including finance, debt, trade, technology and environment).

In terms of action, the leaders agreed that financial experts from their countries should meet and discuss the external debt problem with a view to formulating common approaches.

In the area of trade, and ongoing Uruguay Round, they agreed to "Closely consult each other and co-ordinate our efforts" to achieve a balanced and successful outcome of Uruguay Round which would take into account "the concerns and needs of the developing countries."

In the area of technology, they underscored the importance of improving the access to as well as diffusion and utilisation of new technologies in the South and the need of any regime on intellectual property to effectively promote technological development in the Third World and its access to high technologies. They also agreed to "initiate a significant programme of cooperation in science and technology to enhance the development of the South."

In other areas of joint action, the G-15 agreed on consulting the G-24 (The Third World Group IMF. World Bank institution at Washington) regarding modalities for assisting Third World countries in their dealings with the multilateral financial institutions and in advising Third Word countries on possible effects of the condition imposed by institutions for taking their loans.

G-15 leaders also agreed to hold their summit meeting on an annual basis (the next to be held in 1991—perhaps in June—in Caraces, Venezuela); on the setting up of a Seering Committee on the three Foreign Ministers (from Malaysia, Venezuela and Senegal) for coordinating the work of G-15 until the next summit, and on some institutional support. For the last objective, the Steering Committee was given the mandate to decide on the size and location of a small group of permanent staff to assist it.

With these agreements and a general understanding to act as catalyst or an Action Group of securing South-South cooperation and for affecting North-South relations in a desired way, the G-15 meeting covered a good ground. However, its actual success can be determined by its future role and success with GATT and in resolving other issues of South-South and North-South relations.

Meanwhile the relations between the North and South,

i.e., between the developed and the developing countries, continue to be what these have been since 1970s. The North is continuing its control over international economic system as well as over the economies and policies of the Third World countries.

At the beginning of 1990s, which promises to be a decade of even greater challenges, there are greater prospects of a 'replay" of the adverse factors such as dwindling of financial flows, trade protection and abnormal interest rates. Growth prospects of the major industrial nations are not rated high, at least in the initial years of the decade. There are serious concerns about the trade and economic groupings of powerful nations like the single European Community Market by 1993, US-Canada free trade zone, and other groupings that could follow especially in the event of the failure of the Uruguay round of trade negotiations at the end of 1990.

Experts in global economy have cautioned that the international environment might not be markedly better in the 1990s and the Third World might not regain the growth momentum of the 1950s and 1060s. In regard to resource flows from developed nations, greater attention is now being focused on eastern Europe which is undergoing a total transformation, both political and economic. The reconstruction and adjustments of these countries, shifting their centralised planning to market orientations, could not only be a long drawn out process but also involved the import of massive capital from western nations.

Already there is a competition for savings from richer countries and the surpluses of countries like Japan and Germany. The latter would divert much of its resources to the economy of Germany, while Japanese surpluses will continue to flow, at least in the first half of the decade, to the United States as well as to the countries of East and South-east Asia, that is, mainly the relatively better off developing countries in the category of new industrialising economies (NIEs).

Overall, the global prospects are hardly conducive for the developing countries to continue to adhere to the dependence syndrome.

NAM Economic Committee 1992.

The NAM Economic Committee (1992) Chaired by Indonesian President Suharto has called for democratisation of international relations both in economic and political sectors.

The Economic Committee, did not discuss the Indonesian proposal to establish a committee to deal with the huge debt of the non-aligned countries. The global issues covered related to international economic-co-operation and environment. It has been agreed that conservation of the environment be linked to the eradication of poverty, especially in developing countries.

It has been noted that the successful outcome of the Uruguay Round of multilateral trade negotiations though still uncertain, is a matter of great importance to the developing countries. The principal concern remains the roll back of protectionist measure. The pressure from the industrially advanced countries on issues, such as intellectual property rights must be resisted.

The Committee has strongly urged the producer and consumer countries to make every effort to revive commodity agreements which have lapsed for all products except rubber, because such agreement are not only in the interests of producers, but of consumers as well. It has also urged the signatories to the common fund in the framework of the Integrated programme of commodities to revive the schemes and to make them fully operational. The proposals for the convening of an international conference on commodities with a view to reviewing the principal activity of the common fund was supported.

The committee underlined the need to forge a new, global consensus and commitment to strengthen international economic co-operation for development. It was convinced that international economic cooperation for development can only be fruitful if it is not perceived in terms of demands on the side of the developing countries and charity on the side of the developed ones.

G-15 has launched a few special projects of them, India is the coordination for two: solar energy applications and gene banks for medicinal and aromatic plants. The South Investment, Trade and Technology data Exchange Centre, which was approved at te first G-15 Summit in Kuala Lumpur is already operational. The SIT TDEC data base currently contains over 7,000 documents detailing mainly trade related information.

Greater global interdependence and prolonged economic recession in the North underline the need for South to look to itself to accelerate development and growth. Areas identified for South-South cooperation include the project on bilateral payments arrangements, on population and family planning, self-propelling growth schemes, technical personnel training development of non metallic mineral raw materials, environment mining, river and watershed recovery project.

Dunkel Draft

GATT is a multilateral body that lays down a common code of conduct in international trade and acts as a forum for negotiations and consultations to overcome trade problem and reduce trade barriers. So far seven rounds have been completed and 8th round (Uruguay Round) is under progress.

The Uruguay Round started in 1986. It has a two part

agenda relating to trade in goods and negotiations relating to trade in sources.

During 1990, the progress of negotiations were impeded by serious disagreements, particularly in the following area; (a) the alleged abuse of "anti-dumping" measures to protect the importing country's domestic industry, in contravention of GATT rules, (b) Agricultural trade, (c) Progressive dissolution of multifibre agreement. Talks finally collapsed in Dec. 1990 due to EEC's firm and UN compromising stand on agricultural subsidies. Negotiations again resumed in Feb. 1991.

To break this deadlock Mr. Arthur Dunkel present a draft or Dec. 20, 1991 which contains the substance of discussion of all hitherto disputed points of agenda and required the members to accept it or reject it. There are mainly three areas which require attention.

First, the draft on Trade related Aspects of Intellectual Property Rights (TRIPS) related to the awarding of both product and process patents for all categories of inventions, including areas like drugs and pharmaceuticals. This means, for instance India's existing patent laws need to be changed and it is likely that many existing technological development projects would be abandoned. Article 27 (3) of the TRIPS agreement stipulates that patent should be given micro organism, which will mean to patent life. It will have far reaching consequences on the developing countries.

The second area is agriculture, where the draft seeks to grant of product and process patents to all bio-technological innovations including micro organism, all non-biological and micro-biological process for the production of plant and animals. Thus, the proposal would act as a barrier to the modernisation of agriculture in the developing countries since the local seed companies and formers would be debarred from multiplying seeds and selling them to other farmers.

Under new provisions, the MNCs will have very little compulsion to transfer new technology to the developing countries enterprise.

The third areas is Trade Related Investment Measures (TRIMS) which suggests that developing countries should lift all restrictions on foreign investment. The draft permits foreign firms to refuse granting patent rights and increase to them the access of import of goods. It will mean much worse term for technical collaboration and will lead to reimposition of technological dependency in critical areas. The country would be prohibited from placing any obligations on foreign investors relating to export promotion, use of local component and raw materials and technological transfer requirements.

The Dunkel draft has grave implications for the economic sovereignty and well being of the people in the developing countries. The main concern in the areas, related to TRIPS, TRIMS and GATS. Textiles and agriculture, has been ignored. By bringing all into GATT, the draft has gone beyond the *Puntadel Este* Declaration in promoting the interest of the developed countries.

Instead of self-reliance and indigenous development it opens the way for the unlimited control by MNCs of the economies of the Third World. It reverse the developing countries demand of the 'new international economic order." Moreover, the draft rather than satisfying the needs of the people in the Third World, will impose heavier burden of external debt and debt servicing. The destruction of local technology and small companies and weakening of the country's industrial muscle, will increase misery and unemployment.

The developing countries cannot surrender their right to use the instrument of subsidies to promote particular agricultural crop. The Dunkel draft will obstruct the modernisation and spread the new technology to the various sections of the farmers .in the developing countries.

The successful completion of the Uruguay Round is crucial for the victory of the principle of multilateratlism in International trade and help in facilitating the developing countries demand of the' new international economic order.

Genesis of the New International Economic Order

First, there is the substantial imbalance in the distribution of international monetary reserves. Although Third World nations contained over 70% of the world's population, they received less than 4% of the international reserves of $131 billon during the first a half of the 1970s. Because rich nations control the creation and distribution of these reserves (e.g., through their own monetary expansion and through their effective control over actions of the IMF). They have the power to manipulate these international financial assets to their own benefit.

Second, rich nations benefit disproportionately in the distribution of the value added to the products traded between themselves and the poor nations. Unlike the developed countries. Third World nations receive back only a small fraction of the final price obtained from international purchases of their products. The reason is simple: LDCs are often too weak and powerless to exercise any substantial control over the processing, shipping, and marketing of their primary products. Often they themselves must purchase back at substantially marked-up, prices the final products processed from their own raw materials.

Third, in order to protect and perpetuate profits and jobs in uncompetitive and declining sectors of their economies, rice nations typically resort to tariff and non-tariff protection of inefficient domestic industries while restricting immigration to maintain high wages. Thus, their rhetoric in support of the "free" working of the international market mechanism belies the reality of their market management and control. Third World countries contented, therefore, that any genuine competitive successes they may realise from international trade become nullified by the restrictive commercial policies of increasingly protectionist industrial nations.

Fourth, most of the contracts, leases, and concessions that the multinational corporations have negotiated in the past with the developing countries have unfairly benefited the MNCs at the expense of the host country. Thus LDC host governments contend that because of royalty payments, tax concessions. In addition to political and philosophical writings an important precursor of international organisation has been the practice of multinational conferences, which has parallelled the growth of the nation-state system since the Peace of Westphalia (1648). In the closing phases of the bloody and destructive Thirty years' war (1618-48), assemblies of victorious and vanquished nation-states met for over three years at Osnabruck and Munser (in the German Province of Westphalia) in what came to be referred to as the First European Congress. The result of the war and the protracted negotiations was the èstablishment of the first international balance-of-power system.

8

Globalisation and Development Strategy

The Government has been following the policy of Liberalization, privatization and globalization since 1991. This chapter we will discuss what these terms need for such a till in policies, and how they were initiated, also discuss about World Trade Organization (WTO), which is one of the most important organizations that influences the implementation of new policies and their impact on the Indian economy.

Development Strategy

New policy regime took shape in the 1980s. Its main features were: deregulation of industries, decontrol of prices, liberalization of imports, tax reductions and increase in deficit spending. The contours of this policy regime had emerged immediately after the 1974 low conditionality IMF loan. But the ingredients of this policy seemed temporary as the Janata government tried in vain to modify the pat of development. In any case, it did not crystallize into a coherent package until 1982. The new package was instituted with the IMF loan in 1980 and consolidated in 1985. The logic behind this approach was that the industries which were critically important for the economy, such as coal mining, steel, power and roads, should be retained by the government. It was felt that the government control of critical industries would provide necessary resources to undertake developmental activities in different segments of the economy. The private sector was allowed to establish industries and business enterprises, but was subject to controls and regulations that came in the form of laws. This was also considered necessary, so that resources and wealth would not get concentrated n a few hands. Public sector, the government invested a considerable share of its revenues and started many public sector enterprises. The government outlay in these enterprises increased from Rs. 81.1 crore during the First Five year plan period (1951-56) .to Rs. 34,200 crore during the Ninth five Year Plan period (1997-2002). The purpose behind this strategy was to eliminate poverty, reduce inequalities in the distribution of income and wealth and achieve economic growth with social justice. The continued mobilization of resources led to a situation where India's public sector became very large. Substantial proportion of government revenue went mostly in financing these public sector enterprises, rather than for other developmental purposes.

Bureaucracy and Development

The subject, Administrative Challenges of Planning and Development is of profound significance both for the academic seeking to unravel the developmental phenomenon in societies inhabited by nearly two-thirds of the world's total population and for the country as a whole. At the same time, the subject is multi-dimensional, being amenable to discussion from a variety of angles and perspectives. While not underrating the validity and worth of such disquisitions, the present chapter chooses a somewhat sharp though narrow focus; it seeks to address itself to questions, such as what peculiar challenges public administration in general, and bureaucracy in particular, are likely to face in India in the context of development as embodied in the nation's most authentic developmental blueprint, namely the Fifth Five Year Plan. One should, therefore, turn to the latter to gain a more stable appreciation of the changes demanded in, and challenges encountered by the bureaucracy as well as by the larger political system. The official document entitled "Approach to Fifth Plan (1974-1979)" made only a passing mention of public administration as a factor for consideration in determining the size of the plan including the scale of activities proposed to be taken up during the five-year period. This should be somewhat amazing. As the country has carried out five five-year plans, it is expected of this document to reflect the major experience gained since the launching in 1950, of the First Five Year Plan. Experience has invariably shown that public administration itself has been a severe limiting factor in the implementation of our successive plans. Indeed, as public administration has emphatically emerged as the dominant pipe-line for the carrying out of the policies and programmes, its revealed deficiencies, shortcomings and inadequacies in this respect ought to be of concern to all, more so to the planners themselves. Although the plan document makes a brief mention of this in its concluding part, it is more of a postscript or a tailpiece than an integrated thought. It observes: "An antiquated structure and the leisurely procedures are incompatible with the fulfilment of the plan tasks. Attention needs to be given towards evolving an administrative set-up and modes of functioning which can meet the challenge of the plan. Professionalism in administration must be promoted. The administrator must have capability and the initiative to provide active leadership rather than merely react to the views and actions of others. He must be accountable for results. There is need for visible improvement in the management and operation of the public sector."

Evidently, the plan document does not appear to bestow sufficient thought on administrative imperatives and implications of what it sets out to outline as the basic objectives of the fifth plan. It mostly takes public administration for granted while formulating them; it is assumed that the various objectives visualised in the plan are capable of being accomplished by the existing machinery of public administration. It tends to overlook—or, at any rate, does not recognise—that public administration itself might be a limiting factor in development and could be one of the scarcest resources. Implementability does not seem to be its concern; it has, for that matter, hardly bothered earlier plans either. Not very incorrectly, we as a nation, are sometimes accused of trying to bite more than we can chew!

Inadequacy of the administrative input in the plan could perhaps be explained, to a degree, by the background of the top planners and the highly selective consultation which *Yojana Bhawan* engages in with outside expertise. The Planning Commission is an experts' body, but it includes within its own fold but one kind of expertise—that is, economics. While it is unquestionably true that the economic component of our plan should necessarily be very large, the plan is evidently much more inclusive in its range and character. There are, in addition, distinct administrative, political and sociological dimensions of the plan as well, to mention only a few. The Planning Commission should have, therefore, consciously set out to seek the contribution which these disciplines too are capable of making. None of them has ever found any representation on the Planning Commission. While there has been a panel of economists to advise the Commission on economic aspects of the plan there is none seeking the counsel of other social scientists—political scientists (including students of public administration), sociologists, etc. Not unnaturally, this imparts an impression that there is an absence of awareness in the *Yojana Bhawan* of the possible contribution which these disciplines may make and of its own internal inadequacy in regard to the knowledge in these social sciences in general and public administration in particular. There are, to be sure, professional administrators on the staff of the Planning Commission. But they, as a rule, do not—nor are they expected—to *advise* on the administrative input of the plan. Similarly, the politicians have been associated with the Planning Commission but they, as a class, remain ineviatably engrossed in or pre-occupied with matters relating to the day-to-day politics. At any rate, being practitioners, their almost total passion for individual trees prevents them from acquiring a complete and objective view of the forest, *i.e.*, the social and political system. Those who are outside the wood and have been given to studying it in depth and in a perspective gain a fuller view of the forest than the pure practitioners who are in it.

Nevertheless, the inescapable truth is that no political executive may expect to accomplish more than its public administration permits it to do: it is too much on its part to move much beyond its public administration. Such a realization does not seem to be entirely non-existent in the Government—at least on certain occasions. The Prime Minister, while chiding her partymen for vying with one another in what came to be known as 'competitive radicalism,' queried: "Where is the organisational structure and administrative set-up to implement a more radical policy?" C. Subramaniam, the then Planning Minister, similarly asked: "The question is how far we are in a position to implement a more ambitious plan." Thoughts like these have not become an enduring consideration in determining the scale, variety and pace of our future planning, effort and at the same time compelling us to initiate timely measures calculated to raise and diversify administrative leadership and capability.

The challenging tasks of the 7th plan make exacting demands on public administration, much more on the country's polity. The plan demands total political support and discipline regardless of federal boundaries. Although the present paper is focussed on the administrative aspects of the plan, mention here must be made of the dependence, in multiple ways and in varying intensities, of public administration on the larger system of polity. The political leadership must set an example to others by its devotion to public interest, integrity, hard work, sincerity of purpose, austerity and firmness. As the government in a welfare state inevitably emerges as perhaps the biggest spender of money and dispenser of favours, and an elite glued to these propensities mushrooms threatening to render socialism a topic of public discussion but an instrument of private benefits. This ought to be guarded against. The political leadership must spell out clearly what it would like to accomplish, and in this articulation there must not be left any room for ambiguity or ambivalence. One may also suggest a suitable strengthening, both qualitative and quantitative, of the political wing of the government. Each ministry should have, in addition to the minister, a few junior ministrs, depending upon the nature, variety and volume of work. The political leadership should, with crusader's zeal, address itself to the task of laying down, in full consultation with the civil service, clearly defined policies, preparing time-bound programme compatible with these policies, and overseeing their implementation in accordance with the time-schedule. The point regarding need for utmost clarity in the enunciation of policies cannot be overemphasised. It is fairly well known by now that not much headway could be made in implementing the – much –talked-about land reforms in the country, the failure for this lying not as much in administrative ineptitude as political indecisiveness, irresolution or—which is even more probable—disbelief in the professed programmes themselves. At the same time, public administration can be expected to remain efficient and sensitive to popular aspirations only when it remains under constant political surveillance, control and guidance.

Full realisation of the objectives laid down in the plan document depends, in decisive way, upon the competence, participation and co-operation of all three levels of government in the country—the central, the state as well as the local governments. Although this should look self-evident—it is the age of co-operative federalism—its special mention is absolutely necessary in the present paper in view of not sufficient attention having been bestowed on this aspect in the past. It is absolutely necessary that each plan is firmly backed by an appropriate administrative plan detailing measures of strengthening of the administrative apparatus of the land.

The state level public .dministration is necessarily to be called upon to bear the brunt of the new tasks, and therefore, will have to be considerably strengthened, both in terms of quality and quantity, so that it becomes as apt instrument for undertaking programmes of development. A series of measures are imoerative; the states are well advised to scan the reports of the nearly twenty administrative reforms committees, set up by them from time to time since 1947, and to see that the urgent reforms are swiftly carried out. The well-known tenure system which operates rather erratically at present needs to be enforced more systematically. Not only should a civil servant coming to the central government on a tenure revert to the state (or, service) on his posting after completion of his spell of duty, the tenure system should also be applied in an orderly way within a state itself, ensuring regular exchange of personnel between the field and the headquarters.

Meaningful training in programmes should be organised for state level personnel in various areas to improve their functional proficiency.

Nor should reform of local governments—rural as well as urban –remain shelved, as has generally happened in most states so far. Local government will necessarily have to be involved more meaningfully, more closely and more widely in the efforts at development. It would be good if the states go through the various reports, about twenty in number, having bearing on this subject and quickly implement the necessary reforms.

The seventh Plan more than any that has preceded it, demands a wide range of expertise, and skills in public administration. To recruit persons possessing these and to place them in positions without loss of time, suitable structural changes in the civil service would seem urgently called for. A much larger number of experts and specialists will necessarily have to be inducted into the civil service and their role and place in the generalists-dominated syndrome of bureaucracy has to be appropriately reorganised.

Measures towards enhancement of administrative capabilities at all levels of government and all along the hierarchy must be formulated and put in operation *right now* without any further waiting.

Stress may here be laid on the need for experts and specialists acquiring administrative experience and training to enable them to move into positions of administrative responsibilities in various areas and levels of government.

Bureaucracy, at any rate, a considerable segment of it is under an inescapable obligation to inculcate a disposition towards work in the field—more especially in the rural areas and amongst the vulnerable sections of the population. The rural and the social administrator bears a crucially important responsibility in putting through the various programmes of action. This demands structural and procedural changes in public administration and attitudinal changes in the bureaucracy. A broadening of the social base of the latter would also seem necessary.

As the plan calls for financial resources on an unprecedented scale, the extractive function of public administration—collection of taxes—is to be simultaneously accorded the highest importance. Tax administration at all the three levels of government must needs be streamlined and all possible loopholes—a more appropriate expression would be manholes—be plugged. Also, the prevalent system of financial control, which is evidently out of tune with the needs of a developing economy, stands in need of reform.

Popular urges and aspirations must be continually led into public administration at all levels. Significant in this regard is the need for increased and more meaningful participation of citizens and interest groups in the processes of governmental policy-making and its implementation.

Not the least pressing is the need for economy in public administration. Only one instance might suffice to indicate the gravity of the problem. The expenditure on Administrative services of the Central Government alone was Rs. 21.3 crores in 1950-51; it rose to Rs. 58.7 crores in 1960-61 and Rs. 75.2 crores in 1962-63. It would, thus, be seen that during the period 1950-51 to 1960-61, it galloped by no less than 27.5 percent. This expenditure, registered an increase of as much as 28 percent in just two years—1960-61 to 1962-63. Need a democratic government of one of the poorest countries in the world be necessarily so costly? The National Development Council at one time suggested that the growth of administrative expenditure on tax-collection general administration, etc., should be so controlled as not to exceed five percent per annum. In a sense, it looks rather tropical that the approach paper was published before the third pay commission submitted its report. The third pay commission has announced increase in pay of the central public personnel (including army personnel), which would, almost certainly set in motion similar demands on the part of the government personnel.

Finally and most importantly, political skill and administrative energy should be ceaselessly directed to convert what has been called 'soft state' into 'hard state'. As Gunnar Myrdal observes: "This stands out as significant feature among other conditions that together make a country underdeveloped. Without more social discipline, development will meet great difficulties and, in any case, be delayed. The term 'soft state' is understood to comprise all the various types of social indiscipline which manifest themselves by deficiencies in legislation and in particular law observance and enforcement, a widespread disobedience by public officials on various levels to rules and directives handed down to them, and often their collusion with powerful persons and groups of persons whose conduct they should regulate. Within the concept of the soft state belongs also corruption. These several patterns of behaviour are interrelated in the sense that they permit or even provoke each other in circular causation having cumulative effect."

The present chapter is concluded in the hope and expectation that the administrative aspects, issues and implications of an enterprise would me more carefully analysed and taken care of in the Five Year Plans. This is no less heroic task. Historically, this country has almost always tended to underestimate administration and overestimate objectives, thus lacking faculty to match the two.

Committees for Administrative Reforms

Jha committee reported in the possible scope for replacing direct measures of industrial control by indirect fiscal measures; another Narsimham Committee on industrial licencing and controls pleaded for the simplification of licensing procedures and relaxation of price controls; that on the monetary and credit policy argued in favour of the monetarist rule of a steady growth in money supply; the committee on the black economy showed the link between unreported income, tax evasion and controls; enquiries into the import and export policy considered import restrictions as important bottle-necks of industrial growth and exports and suggested the substitution of physical controls by tariffs for a 'growth-led exports' scenario; and investigations into the public sector suggested that the public sector should conform to the management practices of the private sector. These committees emphasized that the tax structure had become too complex to be effectively implemented, taxes were pitched too high to be realized, administrative controls were too unrealistic to be accepted by the pubic, and the industrial licensing system had become too discretionary to be relevant. They pointed out that the policy regime had become cumbersome and generated black income, and the industrial licensing system and bureaucratic discretion acted as important barriers to industrial growth. These committees also stressed that the public sector, initially designed to create the means of industrialization (power, transport and machines), had not only exhausted its potential, but had also become bureaucratized to the point of constraining industrial growth. It was resource-intensive without the capacity to modernize technology or generate surpluses. Instead of creating the conditions for a self-reliant and self-sustained process of industrial growth, the public sector, it was argued, had become a drag on the economy.

In sum, these committees provided the necessary building blocks for the new economic policy. By 1985 a powerful academic opinion also emerged against the policy regime of controls and regulations. The discussions on the post-

1966 industrial slow-down converged on one aspect, namely, that economic development was inefficient in the sense that the returns on investment were inadequate. The low growth rte of national output, despite a high rate of investment, was attributed to the high capital-output ratio, which implied economic inefficiency. Isher Ahluwalia (1985) and I.G. Patel forcefully argued that the stagnant-high cost-inefficient syndrome was mainly fostered by the regime of subsidies, controls and licences which bred an alliance between the government and various vested interests, that thrived on the exercise of arbitrary power and often operated contrary to the consideration of economic efficiency.

Influential bureaucrats and politicians echoed these: opinions, The PM's closest adviser, L.K. Jha pointed out that the absence of competition was mainly responsible for the steady worsening of the capital-output ratio as well as the slow-down of industrial growth despite the increase in domestic capital. That technological backwardness underlay the industrial stagnation of the 1970s was hardly contested, thought the opinions differed on its causes. A cabinet minister, Vasant Sathe, launched a scathing attack against the public sector. His ire was specifically directed at tits management.

The all-round debunking of the bureaucratic approach to economic growth—through licencing and public sector planning—was accompanied by the emergence of a new technocratic/managerial elite. The Indian government had set up several institutes of management and technology in the late fifties and early sixties. These prestigious institutes turned out graduates who were willing to compete within the Indian private sector and in the world economy. They had entered the public sector as well where the professional ethics they introduced ran counter to state patronage. Thee formally trained managers and technocrats were sharply critical of bureaucratic regulations and controls. It is not fortuitous that Prime Minister Rajiv Gandhi's close friends were not politicians but classmates from the Doon School, who had become businessmen, managers in multinational corporations and advertising executives with managerial and technical skills. They symbolized the rise of professional elites. Some of them might be wheeler-dealers but the majority of them were aspiring entrepreneurs in new fields involving high technology. By the end of 1084, then, verdicts of all official committees were in favour of liberating industries form bureaucratic controls. The intellectual opinion in the country had also veered against the licence-permit raj. In early 1985, significantly enough, several of the erstwhile employees of the IMF and the World Bank became advisers in the Planning Commission, the Ministry of Finance and the Prime Minister's Secretariat. Those who still emphasized the demand constraints on industrial growth were marginalized in policy-making committees.

This strategy has helped India in creating a large industrial base and increase in industrial production. Through poverty and unemployment, which are the twin problems of our economy, have not been eliminated completely. The proportion of population living below poverty line has declined substantially. Earlier, we were importing food grains because we were not able to produce sufficiently enough for all the people. But now, we have become self-sufficient in this field. Besides, a base for export-oriented industries has also been created. India has mobilized savings and has generated its own resources for development. The educational institutions have produced a large pool of scientists and technically skilled working persons. This has helped in industrial and technological growth and self-reliance.

Industrialization did not take place as expected. For instance, when the Indian economy was highly controlled, the growth rate of industrial production was not increasing appreciably. During 1965-1980, the growth rate of industrial production declined to 4 per cent per annum as compared to 8 per cent in 1950-1965. Laws that were formulated to regulate the private sector, were said to be responsible for slow growth of industrial sector. These laws have also failed to reduce he concentration of economic power in the private sector. Corruption, lack of efficiency in work and ineffective management became common features in the public sector enterprises. Many public sector enterprises started making losses. For instance, when the government invested Rs. 18,207 core in 1980-81 towards central public sector enterprises, in lieu of making profits, they incurred losses to the tune of Rs. 203 crore. It was also found that the official machinery, which was created to regulate and run the private sector smoothly had become a major hindrance to its development.

Reforms only the negative aspects that triggered the need for a change in policy, but also several other problems like rising prices, shortage of adequate capital, slow economic development and technological backwardness contributed to it. Government expenditure far exceeded its revenue. By 1991, our borrowings from abroad increased to such a level, that we were finding difficulty in paying even the interests; and we were not able to pay for imports. We had arrived at a severe financial crunch. This financial crisis forced the Indian government to borrow money from international banks such as World Bank and IMF. All these led to the framing of a new policy, which is known as the New Economic Policy, that aims at putting the economy on the track of rapid economic development. The new economic policy contains three strategies – liberalization, privatization and globalization.

Liberalisation contains two components. The first is to allow private sector to run those activities which were restricted earlier only to public sector. The second is relaxation of all the rules and regulations, which had restricted the growth of the private sector earlier. Many industrial activities, which were carried out by public sector enterprises are opened to private sector also. Earlier, a large number of goods, event if they were allowed to be manufactured by private sector. Were required to get prior permission from the government. This system has been abolished for all the goods, except for these: alcohol, cigarettes, hazardous chemicals, industrial explositives, electronic aerospace, and drugs and pharmaceuticals. The number of industries reserved for public sector has been reduced from 17 to 3. Now, private sector can also enter in core industries like iron and steel, electricity, air transport, ship-building, heavy machinery and some defence goods. The private sector has been freed from many regulations such as (a) licensing, (b) permission to import raw materials, (c) regulation on price and distribution, and (d) restriction on investment by large business companies. In fact, many formalities have been simplified to facilitate industrialists to produce goods in India.

Globalisation means integration our economy with the world economy. In this process, we become economically interdependent at the global or international level. This takes place at various levels. Many producers from outside the country can sell their goods and services in India. We can also produce goods and services and sell them in other countries. Globalisation also facilitates those who have capital to establish enterprises in India, produce goods for sale within the country. Or export them in the same way, entrepreneurs from India also can go and invest in other countries. Globalisation includes movement of not only capital, but labourers from one country to other country as well.

Earlier, the Indian government had put restrictions on import of goods to protect domestic producers. These restrictions helped to attain technological capability within the country. The new policy envisages the need for relating the Indian economy with the world economy, so that the unrestricted exchange of capital, technology and experience between countries becomes possible. In pursuance of this policy, the government has removed restrictions on import of goods, reduced taxes taxes on imported goods, and encouraged investors from abroad to invest in India.

The last one decade of liberalisation and globalisation policies in India has led to many visible and invisible changes in the country. Some of the visible changes are: better services in the communications sector, such as telephone facilities, availability of colour television sets and other electronic goods at low prices. Many goof processing companies such as Pepsi, Coca Cola, have entered the country and taken over the market for soft drinks and some food products. Some of the invisible changes in the economy.

India's share in the trade of goods and services in the world has increased marginally. However, compared to other developing countries, our progress is very slow.

Investment from other countries (also known as foreign direct investment) to produce goods and services in India had increased from Rs. 174 crore in 1991 to Rs. 9338 crore in 2000.

We need foreign exchange reserves to pay for our imports. This had increased from for our imports. This had increased from Rs. 4822 crore in 1991 to Rs. 152924 crores in 2000.

The price rise in 1990-91 was about 12 per cent, and it has slowly declined to around 5 per cent in the late 1990s.

One of the objectives of the new policies is to generate employment. Though new jobs are begin created in the economy, it is not sufficient to meet the increasing job requirement in the country. The new policy has failed to generate additional employment where 75 per cent of the population live.

Scheme of Integrated Financial Advisers

In 1976, the scheme of integrated Financial Advisers was introduced in all the ministries in the Central Government. In pursuance of this scheme, Integrated Financial Advisers of the rank of joint secretary or additional secretary have been appointed in the administrative ministries. A Financial Adviser is responsible both to the administrative ministry in which he is posted as well as to the Ministry of Finance. Wider financial powers have simultaneously been delegated to the administrative ministries as part of the scheme of financial reform. The Financial Adviser assists in budget formulation, scrutiny of projects and programmes by the Ministry of Finance. He is also associated with post-budget vigilance to ensure that there are neither considerable short-falls in expenditure nor unforeseen excesses. There is now a close association of Integrated Financial Adviser with the formulation and implementation of all proposals involving expenditure. The Integrated Financial Adviser is also responsible for the preparation of the Ministry's performance budget and the monitoring of progress of various schemes against the budget.

In matters involving any departures from the prevalent budgeting and accounting procedures, consultation with the budget division of the Department of the Economic Affairs (Ministry of Finance) continues to be obligatory. Similarly, respect of the formulation of the concerned ministry's development plans, the Plan Finance Division of the Department of Expenditure is required to be consulted.

Many changes were made in the financial administration of the Central Government in 1976. Since then, the Secretary of a Ministry is the chief accounting authority, and it is he who has to sign the appropriation accounts and ensure preparation of financial accounts of his ministry. The Integrated Financial Adviser, assisted by the circle and pay officers of the ministry, is made responsible, among other things, for keeping entitlement, loan and provident fund accounts. He arranges for the pre-check and payment of all bills by cheques. Maintenance of records relating to payment, reconciliation with banks and final compilation of accounts, etc., is now the responsibility of the ministry, not of the Auditor-General. For the efficient implementation of these financial reforms, a senior officer who has the necessary expertise and knowledge of the civil accounting system and its rules is appointed in each ministry.

Under the new accounting dispensation, the field formations or offices of the different ministries are organised into suitable circles depending upon the nature and volume of work involved. Each circle has one or two more pay officers who are to pre-check all claims and make payments through cheques or demand drafts. They would compile monthly accounts and send them to the Integrated Financial Adviser of the respective ministry. Each ministry has an internal audit cell and although it is organisationally a part of the office of the Integrated Financial Adviser, it is directly under the Secretary of the ministry. The account circles constitute the forward base of the internal audit cells, each ministry, in consultation with the Auditor-General, determines the manner in which its accounts are to be maintained and furnished to the Comptroller and Auditor-General. The ministries also evolve suitable procedures to facilitate the linking of accounts with performance budgeting and performance appraisal.

The Finance Ministry's predominant position manifests itself in other ways as well as the post-budgetary stage. It watches the progress of expenditure in the spending departments through monthly expenditure statements, periodic reports from them, and cautioning them when necessary. Also, it sees that the unspent balances are surrendered by the spending Ministries as early as possible before the close of the financial year. Above all, it gives financial advice and guidance to the spending Ministries generally.

The Finance Ministry's control over expenditure at the execution stage of the budget has come in for a great deal of adverse criticism. The remedy lies in the Administrative Ministries preparing fully detailed schemes at the very outset so that Finance Ministry may give its sanction to them at an early date bringing to minimum the post budgetary checking and control. As Sir Edward Bridges has pointed out in his Stamp Memorial Lectures, 1950, the real function of the Finance Ministry today is to ensure that money is spent in the best way to achieve certain declared objectives, *i.e.*, to ensure the judicious harnessing of resources. Significant is also the following observation of the Planning Commission:

> "A plan of economic development necessarily postulates substantial increase in public expenditure. The importance of securing economy and sound financial control which is already generally recognized is, therefore, further emphasised by the needs of national planning. The objects of financial control are to ensure, (1) that no wastage of resources occurs, (2) that public money is not misapplied, and (3) that for the money spent adequate results are obtained. Within the administration the responsibility for ensuring that these conditions are observed rests equally upon the administrative authorities and upon finance departments, although necessarily, the indent latter have special duties to discharge. There is need always for close co-operation at each level between the financial and the administrative authorities so that, if any difficulties

are encountered, they can be removed through personal consultation at an early stage in the formulation of a proposal and before commitments are entered into. Financial procedures, which, on the one hand, secure adequate control and, on the other, avoid too great an interference in carrying out their own programems, are essential to the efficient execution of the Five Year Plan."

But total elimination of such control is not consistent with the financial accountability of the Government to Parliament.

Trade Unions

AT its 33rd session in 1986, AITUC officials denounced the new policy of denigrating the public sector as dangerous, because it (public sector) 'has been responsible for building a strong industrial base in the core sector leading to self-reliance' and 'plays an objectively progressive role' by creating employment opportunities, promoting regional development, building a self-reliant economy and keeping the multinations at bay. Other trade unions, such as CITU, criticized the policy of economic liberalization more vociferously, attributing it to the weakness rather than the strength of the government. CITU members regarded the scuttling of the public sector as not only bad for workers, but also counter-productive for the Indian capitalist class in the long run since it would further subjugate the country to international capital. Leaving economic development to market forces would gear industrial development to the needs of international capital rather than to those of the Indian people. To express their concern all trade unions, excluding INTUC, organized a convention in October 1986 to oppose the policy of liberalization. On 21 January 1987, 21 lakh workers of the public sector struck work, not for pushing any economic demands but as a political gesture to 'Save Public Sector, Save National Economy.' Another group that opposed the NEP was the left intellectuals. They apprehended as sharp inflow of foreign capital that would undermine the country's autonomy. The World Bank estimated at that time that the seventh Plan would call for a doubling of the gross capital inflow from $17.5 billion to $34.5 billon during the plan period. Since the concessional aid had dried up India was expected to enter into commercial loan commitments of the order of $4.5 billion a year during the plan. The policy of import liberalization was expected to worsen eh position. Under the circumstances, growing external debt was the topmost concern of the participants of seminar organized by the West Bengal government in 1985.

Public sector workers and the leftists were antagonized by the NEP for obvious reasons. But even a section of the ruling party and some industrialists disliked the rabid criticism of the public sector. A cabinet minister, K.K. Tewari called it 'debunking of the Nehru Model.' In May 1985 the Congress Working committee defended the public sector as 'the sheet anchor of India' progress the national instrument for rapid industrialization and for the spread of modern technology into the remotest areas of the country.' And even the PM, who initially endorsed Sathe's vitroic attack on the public sector, spoke up in its defence following the strike of workers. He said, 'The public sector is not an albatross round the people's neck, but an engine of growth and a catalyst of change,' Later at an international conference of public sector executives, he reiterated that 'it is because we invested in the public sector that we have this strength to-day' to question the adverse GATT regulations.

The combined opposition by the public sector workers and left politicians stalemated the NEP by the end of 1986. With regard to fiscal policy the government resorted to pragmatic adjustment and fine turning within the liberalized framework. In the budget of 1987 custom duties on all imports of machinery and capital goods were raised to 85 per cent, the hike for power projects and fertilizers being milder—35 per cent and 15 per cent respectively; profitable zero tax companies were subjected to 30 per cent minimum tax and excise duties were also enhanced.

Foreign Trade

Nevertheless, the process of liberalization continued. Foreign trade was further deregulated with the announcement of three year policy. Despite the deepening deficit in the balance of payments, the OGLlist was enlarged and the import of capital goods was further relaxed. In June 1998 the industries requiring licencing for MRTP/FERA companies from seventy-seven to twenty–six. They were exempt from the licencing requirement if they were established industries is specified backward areas and the investment was less than Rs 50 crores; and in those cases where they set up their units at specified distances outside twenty-one cities, as long as the investment was less than Rs 15 crores. In the following month sixty-nine single product MRTP companies were allowed to diversity (broadband) themselves

Some public enterprises were also integrated with the private sector through the back door. In the field of oil refining. Tata Chemicals collaborated with the Indian Oil Corporation to jointly buildand manage a Rs 1,500 crores oil refinery at Karnal while Indian Rayons of Birlas negotiated tie up with Hindustan petroleum Cooperation to construct and run a Rs 1,200 crores refinery at Mangalore. This was ostensibly done to overcome resource crunch. In 1988 six of the country's largest sector units entered into a minority equity arrangement with a consultancy firm of non-resident Indians based in the US, seemingly for the purposes of technological mordernisation. There were also moves towards the privatization. In 1988 a sick public sector unit, scooter India, was sold off to Bajaj Auto limited; but it seemed like and isolated case.

Thus, despite resistance from trade union and leftists, the public sector was attenuated. Fresh expansion, in the sense of setting up new plants, was foreclosed; the growth of existing units was circumscribed by the availability of internal sources and the quantum of borrowings from the capital market; some companies were integrated with the private sector and a firm was even privatized. In any case, all units were henceforth supposed to emulate the management practices of the private sector. Several public enterprises in fact intensified their in housetraining programmes, where experts from management institutes motivated their middle level managers to adopt 'successful' management practices. While the distinction between the public and private sectors seemed fudged for all practical purposes, full scale privatization was preempted by the resistance of pro-public sector sections such as the organized technocracy and labour aristocracy, backed ideologically by the sizeable, vocal left in the mass media, academia and politics.

The decline of the public sector was accompanied by the growing presence of international capital.

Foreign collaborations jumped from 752 in 1964, itself a record, to 1,024 in 1985 and then tapered off at 957 in 1986 and 853 in 1987, rising again to 926 in 1988. A detailed analysis reveals that thee collaborations continued to increase in seven areas, namely, engineering, consultancy, drugs and pharmaceuticals, food processing, medical and surgical equipments, paper and paper products and information industries. The number of collaborations in these sectors, which apparently benefited from the policy of liberalized import of technology, doubled in three years. Segments in which foreign collaborations sharply increased with the policy announcement buy declined after a year comprised machinery, chemicals, transportation, telecommunications, metal products, textiles, leather and scientific and office equipment. In the remaining industrial areas foreign collaborations declined after the policy announcement. The major collaborators were the USA, West Germany, the UK, Japan and Italy. While the number of collaborations with all these countries shot up in 1985, in the case of Italy and Japan the increase was sustained in 1986 as well. In term of value of foreign investment, the USA not only topped the list, but its rate of investment, the USA not only topped the list, but its rate of investment (approvals) was also sustained up to 19990. West Germany, Italy and Japan stepped up their investment in 1985 and then became cautious.

The economic relations between India and the United States qualitatively improved following, NEP. In three high technology categories—electronics, computers and telecommunications equipment—American exports to India increased by 47 per cent, from $149 million in 1985 to $220 million in 1986. These of course were the very areas in which American multinationals had a keen interest in expanding their business. Their importance to American companies is indicated by the Goldfield Telecommunications Mission, which estimated the Indian telecommunications market at $6-10 billion during the Seventh Plan period. The world telecommunications market was put at $55 billion, of which the US share was about $25 billion.

Emphasising the importance of the changes that took place as a result of the NEP, American ambassador John Gunther dean in a meeting with FICCI on 9 October 1987 said: American corporations have recognized the new business climate in India created by promulgation of more liberal policies and the signing of the Memorandum of Undertaking on transfer of Technology. The US business community has responded with investment. In the past two years

Americans invested more in Indian than they had in the entire previous decade.

Major US companies—many on the leading edge of technology—have entered into many on the leading edge of technology—have entered into collaboration with Indian institutions. The names f these companies have come to be synonymous with the economic dynamism of today's American economy: firms such as Allen-Bradley , Allied Signal, Du Pont, Foxboro, Honeywell, Molex, NCR, Prim Computer, United Technologies, Westinghouse and Xerox. Those are only a few among many.

There are 61 new projects in agriculture alone. Co-operation in space missions presents simultaneously some of our greatest hopes and achievements. The INSAT 1 series of communications satellites, which are American-built to Indian specification, are perhaps the leading example. INSAT IB, which plays a key role in you country's communications, was launched from an American space shuttle. Its backup and successor, INSAT 1C, would have followed the same path into space but for our Challenger tragedy. Despite that setback, we are once again on the road to an important venture. An American firm is now building the advanced Indian-designed INSAT 1D. When it is ready, it will be carried aloft on the first commercial launch of an American Delta rocket.

The United States has provided a supercomputer for monsoon research, which is among the most closely held in the entire range of US high technology. In May 1985 telephone traffic between the United States and India has grown from 700 calls per day to 2,700—far exceeding India's telephone communication with any other country. At officials level we have seen a virtual parade of high-level visits and consultations between representatives of out two countries. Perhaps the most remarkable of these exchanges have come in the areas of a security and defense.

Previously, defence cooperation consisted primarily of a small base of officer exchanges and training programmes. It was only after 1985, and especially after the 1986 visit of Secretary Weinberger, that real progress came. After considerable exploration, the United states approved the sale of an advanced jet fighter engine, the same one used in our top line F-18 Hornet, for use in the development of India's light combat aircraft. We agreed on a 'mission area' approach, under which other component technologies for this project have been approved. Just last month a license was issued so India could acquire a very powerful IBM 3090 computer with appropriate software for use in the design and manufacture of the aircraft a new gas turbine engine for Indian destroyers and specialized radars for other uses. Defense technology teams from India have been given access to some of our most advanced and most sensitive defense production facilities. Where they have seen items of interest, we have opened discussions to see what can be cleared for transfer to India.

These programmes obviously represent only a small corner in the overall picture of the Indian defense establishment. More people are engaged in the process, from cabinet ministers to students and more resources, both public and private, are involved. Thee developments in the space of just two years clearly indicated the extent of India's business relations with the US. They had indeed entered a new phase of growth. Even in the area of defence, where the Soviets had a well-developed niche, the US made a successful bid, shedding tits reservations dating back to the Himalayan war. The black of rapport in this area was decisively terminated in 1986 with enthusiastic tie-ups. Thus, the NEP resulted in (a) arresting the growth of the public sector and (b) integration the national industrial sector, especially its advanced segments, with foreign industries.

Such countries, therefore, have a greater responsibility in controlling damage caused to the environment by the use of such pollution-causing materials. Some of the important measures being considered for this purpose are increased use of renewable and clean sources of energy, less use of fossil fuels. Organic farming, measures to reduce global warming and global limits on carbon emission. Many international agreements have been signed among countries; some of them are the agreement on Environment and agreement on Climate Change and Global Warming. While these agreements seek to protect the interest of the present as well as future generation, under the circumstance it is obligatory on the part of India.

Bibliography

Ajit Kumar Sinha, *New Economic Policy of India*, Deep & Deep Publications, New Delhi.

Alan Blaylock and Edwin H. Duett., The Declining Market Reaction to ADR Issuers in Emerging Markets, Global Business and Finance Review Fall 2004.

Amin, S. (1990), *Delinking: A Polycentric World*, Oxford University Press, New Delhi.

Anderson, Robert J. (1990), 'Reform and Growth: Implications of Trade Reforms for the Growth of the Indian Economy,' A Background World Bank Paper for the 1990 India, Country Economic Reform Memorandum.

Arun K. Datta, *Government, Finance and Capital Market*, P.G. Book Market, Calcutta.

Asif H. Quershi, "The World Trade Organisation: Implementing International Trade Norms," : Manchester University Press, 1996.

Baxi, Upendra, "Global Neighbourhood" and the "Universal Otherhood": Notes on the Report of the Commission on Global Governance, (Manuscript with author) at 12, 1996.

Bagchi, A.K. (1971), "The Theory of Efficient Neo-colonialism," *EPW* (Special Number), July.

Bakke, E. Wright, "Concept of the Social Orgnization," *General Systems*, Vo. IV (1959).

Barach, Arnold B. "U.S.A. and Its Economic Future," *Twentieth*

Century Fund Report. New York: Macmillan Co., 1964.

Banerjee, S. (1984), *India's Simmering Revolution: the Naxalite Uprising*, Zed Books Ltd, London.

Bardhan, P.K. (1973), "On the Incidence of Poverty in Rural Indian in the Sixties,' *EPW*, (Annual Number) February.

Bardhan, P.K. (1978), 'Authoritarianism and democracy: First Anniversary of New Regime,' *EPW*, 18 March.

Baumol, William J. Business Behaviour, Value and Growth, New York: Macmillan Co., 1959.

Bhata, *Indian Economy, Issues and Policies*, Vikas Publishing House, New Delhi.

Bhagwati, J.N. and Desai, P. (1970), *India: Planning for Industrialisation*, Oxford University Press, London.

Bhorali, *GATT Agreement on Dunkel Draft Threaty: Its impact on Agriculture Industry TRIPs and TRIMs and Drug Industry*, Mittal Publications, New Delhi, 1994.

Biswajit Dhar and Sachin Chaturvedi, "WTO Agreements and Agricultural Sector: Implications and Options for India", RITS, New Delhi, 1999.

Buss, Perry, *Marketing and the Behavioural Science*, 2nd ed. Boston: Allyn and BCON, Inc., 1967.

Chandra, N.K. (1973), 'Western Imperialism and India Today,' *EPW*, (Annual Number), February.

Chandrasekhar, C.P. (1988), 'Aspects of Growth and Structural Change in Indian Industry,' *EPW*, (Special Number) November.

Chandler, Alfred D., Jr. Strategy and Structure, Cambridge, Mass.: M.I.T. Press, 1962.

Christopher Arup, "The New World Trade Organisation Agreements: Globalising Law Through Services and Intellectual Property," Cambridge University Press, 2000.

CMIE (1991), World Economy and India' *Place in It*, CMIE, Bombay.

Carr, E.H. *The Twenty Years Crises—A Theory of International Relations*, 1919-1939 2nd ed. London, Macmillan, 1949.

Charles, A. Mecleland, *Theory and the International System*, New York, McMillan, 1966.

Datt, R. (1987), *India's New Economic Policy,* S. Chand & Co., New Delhi.

David Easton, *A System Analysis of Political Life,* New York, John Willey, 1965.

Dev Nathan (191), 'The State,' (mimeo), a paper presented at a seminar, The Problem of Violence, 9-13 September, at the Indian Institute of Advanced Studies, Shimla.

Drengupta, A. (1984), *Report of the Committee to Review Policy for Public Enterprises,* Government of India, Ministry of Finance, New Delhi.

Dutt, R.C. (1969), *Report of the Industrial Licensing Policy Enquiry Committee, Main Report,* Government of India, Ministry of industrial Development, New Delhi.

Ernet. "Discovering the Inner Jones," *Harvard Busines Review,* Vol. XLIII, No. 3 (May-June, 1965).

Fazal, M. (1982), *Report of the Expert Committee of Public Sector Management and Performance,* Government of India, New Delhi.

Ferrer, Robert, And Wales, Hugh, G. (eds). *Motvation and Market Behavoiur,* Homewood, Illinoois: Richard D. (rwin, Inc., 1958.

Fischer D. E. & Jordan R. J., *Security Analysis and Portfolio*

Management, Prentice Hall India, New Delhi.

Ford Foundation (1958), *India's Food Crisis and Steps to Meet It*, New Delhi.

Frankel, F.R. (1978), *India's Political Economy*, 1947-1977, Princeton University Press, Princeton.

Fredrick. L., Schman, *International Politics the Western State System and the World Command*, New York, McGraw Hill 1958.

Ghosh, A. (1992), *Planning in India: The Challenge for the Nineties*, Sage Publications, New Delhi.

Government of West Bengal (1981), *The IMF Loan—Facts and Issues*, Government of West Bengal.

Gottman, J. "Megalopolis: The Urbanized Northeastern Seaboard of he U.S., "*Twentieth Century Fund Report*, New York: Macmillan Co., 1961.

Gokarm.S: Indian Capital Market Reforms, 1992-96, *Economic and Political Weekly*, April13, 1996.

Gupta, S.P. and Raman, P.S. (1992), *Economic Liberalisation and Its Social Impact*, Indian Council for Research in International Economic Relations, New Delhi.

Gupta Shashi K. & Others, *Financial Institutions and Markets*, Kalyani Publishers, New Delhi, India.

Gupta. K.R., *Liberalization and Globalization of Indian Economy*, Atlantic Publishers and Distributors, New Delhi, India.

Gupta. S.P., *Liberalization: It's Impact on the Indian Economy*, Macmillan India, Delhi.

Gupta. L.C., The Changing Structure of Industrial Finance in India, Clarendon Press, Oxford, 1969.

Guruswamy S., *Financial Markets and Institutions*, Vijay Nicole Imprint, Chennai, India.

Haas, E.E. and A.S. Whitling, *Dynamics of International Relations*,

Greenwood, 1995.

Hans, J. Morganthau, *Politics among Nations the Struggle for Power and Peace*, New York, Knoff, 1973.

Harold Nicolson, *Diplomacy,* Oxford University Press, London, 1950.

Harry P. Bower, Abraham Hollander, ad Jean-Marie Viaene: "Applied International Trade Analysis," Macmillan Press Ltd., London, 1998.

Hari Shanker Singhania, "Economic Issues Global & National", Vikas Publishing House Pvt. Ltd., New Delhi, 1995.

Hazari, R.K. (1967), *Industrial Planning and Licensing Policy, Final Report,* Planning Commission, New Delhi.

Henry Ginger, *Diplomacy : How Nations Negotiate,* New York, Harper and Row, 1973.

Holsti, K.J., *International Politics A Framework for Analysis*, Englewood Cliffs, NJ, Printice Hall, 1982.

Herman E. Koenig, "Theory of Modeling Socio-Economic Systems," mimeographed paper. Department of Electrical Engineering, Michigan State University.

Hiro, D. (1976), Inside India To-day, Monthly Review Pres, New York

Hussain, A. (1984), *Report of the Committee on Trade Policies,* Government of India, Ministry of Commerce, New Delhi,

Inis, L. Claude, Jr, *Power and International Relations,* New York, Random House, 1962.

Jain, L.C. (1993), 'Turnaround in Industrial Growth: Hasty Claims for Liberalisation,' *EPW,* 20-27 February.

Jannuzi, F.t. (1989), *India in transition: Issues of Political Economy in a Plural Society,* Orient Longman, New

Delhi.

Jagdish Bhagwati and Mathias Hirsch (Ed.), *The Uruguay Round and Beyond: Essays in Honour of Arthur Dunkel*, The University of Michigan Press, 1998.

Jha, L.K. (1985), *Report of the Economic Administration Reforms Commission on Government and Public Enterprises*, Government of India, Bureau of Public enterprises, New Delhi.

J.M. Clark, "Competition: Static Models and Dynamic Aspects," *American Economic Review*, Vol. XLV, No. 2, May 1955.

Joydeep Biswas, Foreign Portfolios Investments and Stock Market Behavior in a Liberalized Economy: An Indian Experience, *Asian Economic Review*, August Issue 2005,

James, N. Rosenau, *International Politics and Foreign Policy*, New York, 1969.

John Burton, *International Relations: A General Theory*, New York, Cambridge University Press, 1965.

John-N. Herz, *International Politics in the Atomic Age*, New York, Columbia University Press, 1962.

Jehsen, L, *Explaining Foreign Policy*, Englewood Cliffs, NJ Printice Hall, 1982.

Karanjia, R.K. (1975), *Indira-JP Confrontation: The Great Debate*, R.K. Karanjia, New Delhi.

Katona, George, "Rational Behaviour and Economic Behaviour," *Psychological Reveiw*, Vol. LX, No. 5 (September, 1953).

Karl, W. Deutsch, *The Nerves of Government Models of Political Communication and Control*, New York, Free Press, 1966.

Kenneth Waltz, *Man, The State and War A Theoretical Analysis*, New

York, Columbia University Press, 1965.

Kelley, Eugene J.: Lazo,Hector: Corbin, Arold:and Kahn, Edward. *Marketing Management: An Annotated Biblioraphy,* Chicago: american Mrketing Associiton, 1963.

Lewis, J.P. (1970), 'Wanted in India: A Relevant Radicalism,' EPW (Special Number0, July: also reprinted in C.D. Wadhwa, ed., *Some Problems of India's Economic Policy,* Tata McGraw-Hill, New Delhi, 1973).

Little, I., Scitovsky, T. and Scott, M. (1970), *Industry and Trade in Some Developing Countries: A Comparative Study,* Oxford University Press, London.

L.M. Bhole and Shreeya Pattanaik. The State of Indian Stock Market Under Liberalization, *Finance India,* Vol. XVI No.1, March 2002.

Marathe, S.S. (1986), *Industrial Policy in India—Retrospect and Prospect,* Sage Publications, New Delhi.

Malineau, Pierre, "Social Class and Spending Behaviour," *Journal of Marketing,* Vol. 23, No. 2 (October, 1958).

M. Francesco, Consumer Decision Processes: Marketing and Advertising Implications, Englewood Cliffs, New Jersey:Prentie-Hall, Inc., 1966.

Morton, A.. Kaplan, *New Approaches to International Relations,* New York, St. Martin,1968.

Mundle, S. (1992), 'Employment Effects of Stabilisation and Related Policy Changes in India, 1991-92to 1992-93' in ILO-ARTEP, *Social Dimensions of Structural Adjustment in India,* New Delhi.

Myrdal, G. (1954), *Economic Theory and Underdeveloped Regions,* Orient Longman, New Delhi.

Nagaraj, R. (1990), 'Growth Rate of India's GDP, 1950-51 to 1987-88): Examination of Alternative Hypotheses,'

EPW, 30 June

Nair, K.R.G. (1982), *Regional Experience in Developing Economy*, Wiley Eastern, New Delhi.

Narasimhan, M. (1985), *Report of the Committee to Examine Principles of Possible Shift from Physical to Financial Controls*, Government of India, New Delhi.

Nayar, B.R. (1989), *India's Mixed Economy*, Popular Prakashan, Bombay.

Nayar, B.R. (1990), *The Political Economy of India's Public Sector: Policy and Performance*, Popular Prakashan, Bombay.

Nayar, D. (181), The IMF Loan and Its Conditions' in Government of west Bengal, The IMF Loan—Facts and Issues, Government of West Bengal, Calcutta.

Nayyar, K. (1971), *India: The Critical Years*, Vikas, New Delhi,

Neri, M. 9190), 'Abrasive Beginning,' *The Illustrated Weekly*, 15 July.

N.K.P. Sinha & M.B. Singh, "Industrial Development in India", Rawat Publications, New Delhi, 1993.

Patel, I.G., (1987), 'Free Enterprise in the Nehru Era,' in D. Tripathi, ed., *State and Business in India*, Manohar Publications, New Delhi.

Pettman, R., *Human Behaviour and World Politics, An Introduction to International Relations*, New York, St Martin's, Press, 1975

Planning Commission (1969), *Fourth Five Year Plan*, Government of India, New Delhi.

Purshottamdas Thakurdas (1944), *A Plan of Economic Development*, New Book Company.

Rao, V.K.R.V. (1983), *India's National Income*, 1950-80, Sage publications, New Delhi.

Sathe, V. (1987), "Planning Process and New Directions of Policy" in R. Datt, India's *New Economic Policy*, S. Chand & Co., New Delhi.

Sen, A. (1990), 'How Is India Doing?' in Chaudhury, R.A., Gamkhar, S. and Ghose, A., *The Indian Economy and Its Performance Since Independence*, Oxford University Press, New Delhi.

S.K. Misra & V.K. Puri, *Indian Economy - Its Development Experience*, Himalaya Publishing House.

Seshan, A. (187), *Burden of Domestic Public Debt in India*, Occasional Paper, Reserve Bank of India, Bombay.

Sidharthan, N.S. (1981), *Technology, Market Structure and the Decentralisation in the Growth of Capital Stock in the Indian Engineering Industries*, Institute of Economic Growth, New Delhi.

Singh, B.P. (1983), *Retrospect and Prospect of Indian Agriculture*, Federation of Indian Chambers of Commerce and Industry, New Delhi.

Swamy, D.S. (1980), *Multinational Corporations and The World Economy*, Alps International, New Delhi.

Tangermann, Kessing's Record of World Events, 1994-Except from Gill, Gerald J, *Nepal's Agricultural Trade in the New World Trading Order* , 1996.

UmaKapila, *Indian Economy Since Independence: The Ongoing Economic Reforms*, Delhi Academic Foundation.

Uruguay Round, Consolidating Economic Globalisation, (address by Peter Sutherland, to the Canadian Clumb Toronto), New of the Uruguay Round, NUR 083, 22nd March, 1994.

Various reports of the World Trade Organisation (WTO),

Varghese, *Indian Economy Problems & Prospects*, Ashish Publishing House, New Delhi.

Venkata Subramanian. K., *Policy and Performance of Indian Economy,* Manoj Prakasham Publications, Bangalore, India.

Vinod Vyasulu Hemalata Rao, *Indian Economy: Emerging Challenges,* Printwell, Jaipur, India.

Vernon-V. Dyke, *International Politics,* New York, Appleton-Century Crofts, 1957.

Wright, Q. *The Study of International Relations,* New York, Irvington, 1984.A.H. Maslow, *Motivation and Personality* (New York: Harper & Row, Publishers, 1954).

Weiner, M. (1989), *The Indian Paradox,* Sage Publications, New Delhi.

World Bank, *World Development Report,* 1987, and 1992.

Index

***